ADVANCE PRAISE FOR

Radical Saints

Each person has a radical call to holiness to the point of sainthood. How can that be in this day and in this age? God never asks the impossible; Melanie Rigney has given us twenty-one radical women who prove the feasibility of such a call. What joy the reader will encounter as they revisit familiar saints, while learning new facts and being inspired in ways to holiness in their own lives while also discovering new friends. Radical Saints offers a format of biography, reflection, question, and resources, that is perfect for individual or small group study.

—ALLISON GINGRAS, www.reconciledtoyou.com and *The Stay Connected Journals for Catholic Women: The Gift of Invitation*

I immersed myself in these stories about ordinary women living extraordinary lives; the reflections on "Living Radically Today" were as insightful as the saints themselves. Thank you for providing the next book club selection for our group!

—JEAN KELLY, president, National Council of Catholic Women

The path to sainthood is varied for every individual, but a few common virtues and traits are shared by every saint: holiness, strength, and courage. Melanie Rigney, a great resource on the lives of holy women, proposes that many saints are also "radicals" in the very best sense of the word. Join Rigney for a new perspective on the lives of many well-known saints and an introduction to new spiritual giants to accompany you on your own journey of radical love and faith.

—LISA M. HENDEY, author of *I'm a Saint in the Making*

Melanie Rigney introduces 21 saints who endured much and persevered in their commitment to God's call in their lives. What makes these saints radical is not extreme beliefs or practices; it's simply that they chose to love God and their neighbor without reserve. Anecdotes about Melanie's contemporaries who embody the same values as these saints reinforce the concept that everyday women can embody the same gifts that the saints do. Let the radical saints of the 20th century inspire you to face the challenges in your lifetime.

—BARB SZYSZKIEWICZ, editor, CatholicMom.com;
managing editor, *Today's Catholic Teacher*

When we think of "radical" women, we might conjure up images of screaming women with pink hats waving signs with political slogans. Or female talk show hosts, angry at a guest they don't agree with. Melanie Rigney has gathered together 21 radical women who through their Catholic faith will change that image for you. *Radical Saints: 21 Women for the 21st Century* is a compilation of 21 extraordinary women who lived their faith in the most radical terms by not caring what the world thought of them. In her latest book, Melanie has brought to life Catholic women of all ages who are real examples of what radicalism can mean.

—PAM SPANO, Being Catholic… Really, CatholicMom.com,
and Catholic365.com writer

Radical Saints

21 Women
for the
21st Century

Melanie Rigney

franciscan
media
Cincinnati, Ohio

Cover and book design by Mark Sullivan

Published by Franciscan Media
28 W. Liberty St.
Cincinnati, OH 45202
www.FranciscanMedia.org

Printed in the United States of America.
Printed on acid-free paper.
20 21 22 23 24   5 4 3 2

Radical.

The word makes us, well, itchy. We think of people whose political beliefs are at one end of the spectrum or the other, people who won't compromise or collaborate, maybe even people who foster revolutions that upset entire nations.

How in the world could a group of women, ranging in age from nine to ninety-three at their deaths, women formally canonized by the Catholic Church for heroic virtues and associated miracles, be considered radical?

Because being a Christian *is* radical. The word *radical* comes from the Latin *radicalis,* meaning "of or relating to a root." When Christ and his teachings are our foundation, we are on a radical path, a path people have struggled to walk for more than two thousand years. Think about it: Is there anything more radical than loving God with your entire being and loving your neighbor as yourself? Society encourages us to worship money, status, prestige, and more. Putting God before any of that? Before our own spouses, parents, children, friends, all those people we love and would do anything for? And how about loving those who look different from us or who have betrayed us, injured us, or persecuted us simply because we're told God loves them every bit as much as he loves us?

Now *that's* radical.

"I came to bring fire to the earth, and how I wish it were already kindled!" Jesus told the disciples (Luke 12:49). These women, from Dulce to Faustina, got that. They lived it, and they didn't care whether it cost them earthly love or respect.

They did so in a world that looked much like ours. All twenty-one saints featured in this book walked the earth in the twentieth century and were canonized in the twenty-first. (By the way, that's why Zélie Martin, who died in 1877 and was canonized in 2015, and Teresa Benedicta of the Cross, who died in 1942 and was canonized in 1998, aren't in this book. We had to draw the line somewhere.)

Many of these saints took trains, rode in cars or airplanes, received telegrams, talked on phones, watched television and movies, and perhaps a few knew their way around a computer. All were photographed, and many were filmed as they shared their radicalness. They had an awareness of some—not all, but some—of the modern-day distractions that, when not used in moderation, threaten to crowd out room for God. And while they may not have taken selfies and had social media accounts, I think it's a pretty safe bet that if they had, they wouldn't have been checking likes and shares at prayer, meals, or time with their loved ones.

I'm not saying that any saint from the Blessed Virgin Mary on had an easy life. Some joys and sorrows—the birth of a child, the loss of a spouse—are eternal. Some, such as martyrdom, are difficult for people living in any age to imagine. We can learn something from each and every one of our beautiful saints regardless of the century; indeed, the women in these pages were inspired by Teresa of Ávila, Thérèse of Lisieux, Bridget of Sweden, and others. Still, there's something especially moving and challenging about the faith and perseverance of women who actually walked the earth with us or our mothers or grandmothers.

In each chapter, you'll find brief descriptions of the woman's radical gift and the world in which she lived. You'll learn more about how she lived radically and find some relevant Scripture and questions for journaling or discussion, along with resources if you'd like to learn more about her.

Just as important, you'll find the true stories (in some cases, with names changed) of "everyday" women who are living these gifts in ways large and small today. Sometimes I'll share stories about the way my life has been changed by an experience or by knowing one of them. Sometimes the pairings might surprise you—for example, a schoolteacher living Gianna Beretta Molla's selflessness or a mom of two illumining the vocational devotion of a longtime Carmelite. Every one of them is extraordinary in her ordinariness.

You know people who are living radically too. And I'm sure people think the same of you as they watch the way you trust, suffer, accept, and more, consciously or unconsciously. You think it's no big deal, just like the women in this book did and do. But I assure you it is.

You see, it's easier to be radical than we think. All we have to do is stop playing it safe—and follow the leader.

CHAPTER I

Irmã Dulce Lopes Pontes
Turning Empathy into Action

The Basics

Born May 26, 1914, in Brazil | Died March 13, 1992, in Brazil
Canonized October 13, 2019 | Feast Day: August 13

Dulce's Radical Gift

St. Dulce was nominated twice for the Nobel Peace Prize. Most of her sixty years of serving the poor was done in her hometown. Dulce shows us that sometimes the most radical way to change the world is to bloom where we are planted.

Dulce's World

In her lifetime, Dulce's hometown in northeast Brazil grew from less than 300,000 people to more than a million. The country experienced a number of changes in political leadership and endured twenty years of military dictatorship. Questions arose as to whether Brazil's papal nuncio had spied for the Axis during World War II. When St. John Paul II visited in 1980, hundreds of thousands of people turned out.

Dulce's Radical Path to Holiness

Dulce was born Maria Rita de Souza Brito Lopes Pontes. She was just thirteen the day one of her aunts took her into some of the poorer neighborhoods in her hometown of Salvador. It wasn't unusual for the girl to spend a day with a relative; Maria's mother, Dulce, had died when the child was just six, and extended family had been very involved in helping her father, a dentist, raise Maria and her four siblings.

We have no record of what, specifically, Maria saw that day, but we can imagine. One of Brazil's literary classics about the time, the novel *Captains of the Sands,* talks of orphan gangs living on Salvador's streets. A good share of the population lived in slums known as *favelas,* often without the basic necessities of food, sanitation, shelter, and clothing.

Some of us see similar images on a regular basis, on the news or in our own cities and neighborhoods. Grime, disease, and all the other aspects of poverty make us uncomfortable. We may express sorrow or indignation when we talk with our friends; give a bit more money to a diocesan or nonprofit appeal as a result; or offer up prayers. But prayers go only so far when you haven't had a decent meal for three days, or your mother has a cough that's just not getting better.

Even though she was just thirteen, Maria did more than pray. She sprang into action. The next thing anyone knew, she had started taking people into her family's home to care for them. She took another step a couple years later and attempted to join a religious community, believing that was how she was called to serve God and his people. But she was denied because of her age.

Finally, when she turned eighteen, the young woman entered the Congregation of the Missionary Sisters of the Immaculate Conception (SMIC). She would be known as Sister Dulce, her mother's name. For the next sixty years, Sister Dulce would be a tireless advocate for Brazilians living on society's margins, in particular in her hometown. There was nothing she would not do to help them, including physically carrying people to the hospital—even during her final thirty years when her lung capacity was a fraction of a healthy person's.

Her body of work is dizzying, mind-boggling. Small wonder Dulce became known as "the good angel of Bahia." She founded an organization for workers, a clinic for the poor, and a school for working families. She established an orphanage and care centers. Dulce did all of this in a very active way, not from behind a desk in a convent office. For example, when she was in her thirties, she set up housekeeping with seventy sick people, but they all were booted from the neighborhood. Then she tried moving the group into an old fish market, but they were evicted from that structure as well. Finally, she asked her mother superior for use of the community's chicken coop. Dulce got permission, with the caveat that she tend the chickens. She did that by turning them into meals for her little band. Today a hospital stands where the coop once did.

Dulce slept only a few hours a night, often wandering the streets after dark to look for people who needed medical care desperately but couldn't afford it.

The honors rolled in: two Nobel Peace Prize nominations. Two personal audiences in Brazil with St. John Paul II. At the first audience, the pope thanked her for all her work but urged her to slow down a little; the second audience was not long before she died. After her death, she was recognized as Brazil's most admired woman in history and as the most influential religious person in her country in the twentieth century.

Obras Sociais Irmã Dulce, or the Charitable Works Foundation of Sister Dulce, was formally established in 1959, and today it consists of hospitals, clinics, schools, and more. More than two million outpatient procedures are performed at the medical facilities each year.

DULCE'S WISDOM

"The important thing is to do charity, not to talk about charity. We must understand the work with very poor people as a God's chosen mission."[1]

LIVING RADICALLY TODAY

We admire Dulce and missionaries like her who bring the Lord to the sick, the dying, and the poor. But emulating them seems much harder. We have parents and spouses and children and grandchildren to care for. We have jobs that eat up a good share of our days and brains. It's just not feasible for most of us to leave all that behind.

But like Dulce, we can be present to the person in front of us, whether that person is a family member, a friend, a colleague, or someone we'll never see again. Sometimes that assistance will involve services or money; many times it's about a hug or a smile or a word or small act of kindness.

Let me tell you about a member of Dulce's congregation. Her name is Sister Jane, and she's been an SMIC since 1960. While she's been a missionary in the United States, Taiwan, and the Philippines, it was in a small western Pennsylvania community at a writers' conference that I met her. At mealtimes, Sister Jane ate homemade snacks in her car. I'm not sure where she slept. She had cheerily brushed aside the offer of a scholarship, saying someone else could put the gift to better use.

My birthday happened to fall during the conference. It was my first birthday since returning to the Catholic Church after thirty-three years away. I told Sister Jane that I was spending lots of hours volunteering and reading and trying to make up for lost time. She listened, then said she had a gift for me. I figured we were going to say a Rosary together.

Instead, we got into her car and drove to a Catholic church. "We're going to Adoration," Sister Jane said, beaming, as she parked the car.

I gulped. "What will we do? I don't even know what Adoration is."

She smiled again. "Just be quiet with Jesus for an hour."

So in we went. I knelt, thinking I'd say an Our Father or two and then read the hymnal for fifty-eight minutes. But the next thing I knew, Sister Jane was tapping me on my shoulder. I looked at my watch. An hour had passed.

These days, I'm kind of an Adoration junkie. I switched parishes to attend one that offered more Adoration hours. I go before Mass each week, and I've been on Adoration teams. Adoration is the best place for me to shut out the noise in the world and in my head and simply be quiet with Jesus.

Sister Jane saw that I was starving spiritually. She could have merely suggested that I spend some time in silence or recommended some resources. But instead she ministered directly to me. We can do the same, every day, in small ways, for those we encounter, starting at home.

RADICAL THOUGHTS

Here are a couple of verses to contemplate as you think about Dulce's life:

"Plant your people in your holy place, as Moses promised" (2 Maccabees 1:29).

"Return to your home, and declare how much God has done for you" (Luke 8:39).

Consider journaling about the following questions, or use them to spark discussion with a group of friends:

- Do you sometimes feel "less than" friends from high school or college who have moved away and have seemingly glamorous lives? How can you put aside those feelings of envy and serve where you are?
- Conversely, if you're the one who has moved away, consider expressing admiration for someone who stayed put and is doing good.
- Visit a new-to-you neighborhood in your town. Can your "fresh eyes" identify something you can do to help the residents?

Praying with Dulce

St. Dulce, help me to open my eyes to the Christ inside everyone I encounter today and to take whatever action I can to reflect his love.

Resources

- View a video about Bahia, where Dulce lived and worked.
- Learn more about the ongoing work of Obras Sociais Irmã Dulce.
- See images of Dulce (including one with St. Teresa of Calcutta) at the Postulator of the Causes of Saints site.

CHAPTER 2

Mariam Thresia Chiramel Mankidiyan
Accepting God's Unexpected Gifts

The Basics
Born April 26, 1876, in India | Died June 8, 1926, in India
Canonized October 13, 2019 | Feast Day: June 8

Mariam Thresia's Radical Gift
St. Mariam was beset by demons, criticized for direct service to the needy, and thwarted for a time in her quest to become a woman religious. Her steadfast faith kept her on the path God mapped out for her, even when others attempted to redirect her.

Mariam Thresia's World
Much of India was under British rule throughout Mariam Thresia's life. Kerala, the state in which she resided, is on the country's southwest coast. The region was the site of uprisings that cost thousands of lives. The Syro-Malabar Catholic Church, of which she was a member, is in full communion with Rome and had undergone some reorganization under Pope Leo XIII when Mariam Thresia was a child.

Mariam Thresia's Radical Path to Holiness
It's the rare saint who had an easy life. Especially for a modern-era woman, however, Mariam Thresia's years were fraught with difficulty, including repeated exorcisms.

She was named Teresa, for St. Teresa of Ávila, but midway through her life, she asked to be called Mariam, for the Blessed Virgin Mary. Even as a child, Mariam Thresia exhibited behaviors some thought were extreme. Later, she would tell her spiritual director that during this time she offered mortifications that included severe fasts, lying without a mat on pebbles and glass pieces, and kneeling on gravel as she prayed.

Her family life was challenging as well; her father was left all but destitute after providing marriage dowries for his seven sisters and his other two daughters, and he was given to drinking. Mariam Thresia, the third child, decided to consecrate herself to Jesus as a virgin at an early age.

Mariam Thresia's mother died when she was twelve, and the girl's rudimentary education ended then. Three years later, Mariam Thresia came up with a plan to move into the woods and live as a hermit, but she was unable to do so—perhaps because of divine intervention. Her next step was even more controversial for a woman of her day: She and three friends, without a male chaperone, began caring for orphans and the sick—including those suffering from Hansen's disease, then known as leprosy. The women were roundly criticized for these audacities but continued their ministry. Around the same time, Mariam Thresia began experiencing ecstasies and visions, which confused her greatly. How distressed she must have felt, wondering whether she was doing what the Lord desired or was being punished for some misdeed!

The spiritual assistance she prayed for came when she would need it most. She attended a retreat in 1902, and Father Joseph Vithayathil was among those hearing confessions. During confession, Miriam asked if he would be her spiritual director, but he declined. A few months later, he was transferred to her parish, where she repeated the request. This time he said yes, and he would remain her spiritual director until her death.

The worst of Mariam Thresia's experiences with evil spirits had begun that January and lasted for three years. People would come to see her hanging on a wall in her room in a way similar to the crucifixion. She reported wounds and the temporary severing of her extremities. She said she was tortured while praying. Food was taken from her as she attempted to eat. Some observers confirmed these events, which troubled authorities to the point that Mariam Thresia experienced several exorcisms. How much occurred due to some sort of mental impairment rather than demons, we will never know.

Amid all this tumult, Mariam Thresia expressed the desire to begin a retreat house, but the effort was rejected by her bishop. He suggested instead that she become a Poor Clare, then a Carmelite. Neither proved to be a good fit.

Finally, in 1913, after leaving the Carmelites, Mariam Thresia received permission to create a house of prayer. Within a year, she and Father Vithayathil founded the Congregation of the Holy Family. Three childhood friends joined her as postulants. Finally, even though some of her challenges continued, Mariam Thresia's patience and trust had been tangibly rewarded. In the next twelve years before her death due to complications of diabetes, Mariam Thresia saw the congregation grow to include additional convents as well as schools and an orphanage.

At her beatification in 2000, St. John Paul II said, "Sister Mariam Thresia's willingness to embrace the Cross of Christ enabled her to remain steadfast in the face of frequent misunderstandings and severe spiritual trials."[2]

MARIAM THRESIA'S WISDOM

"God will give eternal life to those who convert sinners and bring them to the right path."[3]

LIVING RADICALLY TODAY

My friend Lynn was a teenager when she took her first painting lessons. Even then she loved the tactile experience of mixing colors, of putting them on media. Painting—and pretty much anything else that involved working with her hands—brought her joy.

Lynn never put away her paints entirely, not when she moved thousands of miles away to college; not when sudden and tragic death struck her large family of origin; not when she married and moved with her husband all around the world. Painting helped her through struggles with infertility and the odyssey that led them to adopt their son. But it was a private joy, a form of spiritual therapy; while many of Lynn's friends knew she painted, few of us had seen any of her work beyond amazing banners for her favorite ministry. Painting helped her with her private struggles and more public ones, such as when a pastoral change caused such upheaval at the parish she'd attended since she was a child that it resulted in a search for a new spiritual home.

As their son entered his teens, Lynn and her husband were challenged to find the right school for him. He's bright but easily bored, and you know how bored teenagers behave. After several attempts, they settled on a nontraditional school. There was just one challenge: It was a long way from their home. That would mean a minimum of three hours of Lynn being on the road each and every weekday. Lynn and her husband were committed to their son's success, but it would be a lot of wear and tear on her, not to mention her vehicle. But she couldn't exactly drive him to school in the morning and hang out in the car until classes ended either.

They decided that not only was their son's education worth an investment, so was Lynn's painting. They rented a place near the school for her to set up a studio. Their son is thriving in his school, and Lynn is thriving in her artistic gifts. They were always there, but now they are bubbling to the top. A couple of years ago, this fifty-something introvert found the courage to establish her own business, and she now sells more than a dozen varieties of cards bearing her work, most with spiritual messages. She also has exhibited her artwork at conferences.

Now, to my knowledge, Lynn has never experienced evil in the paralyzing way that Mariam Thresia did. But I do know that, like me, she has struggled with overeating. She's struggled with balancing her responsibilities as a wife, mother, and daughter, and with people seeming to judge her by the same yardstick as her outgoing mother. But through it all, Lynn has remained steadfast in her faith and honored the artistic gifts God has given her. These days, she's doing it more publicly. She also smiles and laughs a lot more than she used to.

RADICAL THOUGHTS

Here are a couple of verses to contemplate as you think about Mariam Thresia's life:

> "Then he said to them all, 'If any want to become my followers, let them deny themselves and take up their cross daily and follow me'" (Luke 9:23).

> "Rejoice in hope, be patient in suffering, persevere in prayer" (Romans 12:12).

Consider journaling about the following questions, or use them to spark discussion with a group of friends:

- Evil exists in this world in many forms—some of them very attractive. What can you learn from Mariam Thresia's experience to combat it?

- Is there an activity that draws you closer to God—painting, perhaps, or writing or gardening or cooking? How can you intertwine it more deeply with your spiritual life?

Praying with Mariam Thresia

St. Mariam Thresia, be with me as I gently set aside society's judgments and measurements of me. Help me to always be steadfast in my faith as I grow ever closer to the Lord.

Resources

- Visit the Mariam Thresia Pilgrim Center site, which features information about her life and other resources.
- The Congregation of the Holy Family site, in addition to featuring biographies of Miriam Thresia and Father Joseph Vithayathil, shows how the sisters continue to work today.
- See the New Delhi TV (NDTV) coverage of this saint's canonization.

CHAPTER 3

GIUSEPPINA VANNINI
Fiercely Persistent

THE BASICS

Born July 7, 1859, in Italy | Died February 23, 1911, in Italy
Canonized October 13, 2019 | Feast Day: February 23

GIUSEPPINA'S RADICAL GIFT

Women in the religious community who had all but raised her didn't think St. Giuseppina was cut out for their life, rejecting her twice. But Giuseppina persisted in her vocation, and ultimately she cofounded and led a community, the Daughters of St. Camillus.

GIUSEPPINA'S WORLD

Italy and the Papal States were in turmoil throughout Giuseppina's life. Rome, her birthplace, was declared the capital of the unified Italian kingdom in 1861 even though it was still under the pope's control. Leo XIII was pope for most of her adulthood; he has the distinction of being the first pope for whom we have audio and video recordings.

GIUSEPPINA'S RADICAL PATH TO HOLINESS

It was perhaps logical that the girl born Giuditta Adelaide Agata would believe she was destined for the religious life. After all, the Daughters of Charity of St. Vincent de Paul in her hometown were her primary role models. Giuditta's father had died shortly after her fourth birthday; her mother died when she was seven. She and her siblings were split up, her brother moving in with relatives, and her sister going to a different religious community.

Giuditta studied to teach kindergarten, but at age twenty-four she became a novice at the Daughters of Charity in Siena, 150 miles away. After four years, she was sent back to Rome to recover from some health issues. A year later, she tried to resume religious life in Siena but was told that her health (and perhaps her quiet, shy personality) made her unsuitable. It's easy to imagine her reaction, whether she showed it to others or not. The sisters had taken her in when she had no one else. And now they were rejecting her? What could God have in store for her, if not the life she knew?

About three years passed. What Giuditta was doing during this period is unclear. What we do know, however, is that in December 1891, she went on a retreat that changed everything. She was on one side of the confessional, talking about the need for the Lord's direction; on the other side was Father Luigi Tezza. Father Tezza was fifty-six years old and had joined the Camillian order when he was just fifteen. The Camillians, founded in 1582 by St. Camillus de Lellis, minister to the sick. (Their distinctive red cross emblem precedes by nearly three hundred years the founding of the American Red Cross.) Father Tezza had been thinking of forming a community for women religious to support those in need, and he asked Giuditta to discern whether that was her vocation. It didn't take long for her to say yes.

She and two other women became lay members the following year, and by the end of December 1895, the Daughters of St. Camillus was born, with Giuditta—now known as Giuseppina—as superior general.

Father Tezza was sent to Peru in 1900, possibly due in part to unfounded rumors about his relationship with the sisters. That left Giuseppina in charge of the fledgling community that had yet to receive formal papal approval. (The approval wouldn't come until twenty years after her death.) But undeterred by Father Tezza's absence or the lack of official authority, the Daughters' ministry under her leadership expanded to France, Belgium, and Argentina.

Giuseppina was beatified by St. John Paul II on October 16, 1991; Father Tezza's beatification followed on November 4, 2001. At her beatification, the pope said she "invites to generous correspondence both those who are called to consecrated life and those who realize their vocation in family life: above all, God has a plan of holiness."[4]

The sisters continue their work today in eighteen countries in Asia, Africa, Europe, and South America. Like Giuseppina, they vow to serve the sick and poor, even at risk to their own lives.

Giuseppina's Wisdom

"Take heart! First of all it is God who sends things forward and not me. And then from paradise I can do more than I do in this world. When I will no longer be, believe also that it will be better than it is done now."[5] (Her deathbed words)

Living Radically Today

Giuseppina's life was full of change, and much of it less than pleasant to the human eye. Yet she accepted it and stayed on course.

Unlike Giuseppina, I'm someone who can give up pretty quickly, mainly because I dread conflict, especially external. When a situation gets hard, I tend to tell myself that it wasn't God's plan and start pursuing Plan B. Sometimes that's the right thing because Plan A was my plan, not his. Other times, not so much.

A few years ago, I was put in charge of a church-related communications committee, a committee three people in particular didn't think I was qualified to lead. Well-meaning mutual friends told me what was being whispered about my shortcomings. After feeling sandbagged at a meeting less than six months into the position, I went to the ministry director to quit. Instead of accepting my resignation or agreeing that I was being persecuted, she told me to pray about why what was being said, rightly or wrongly, mattered so much to me. She encouraged me to talk with the people who were critical of me.

And while those conversations didn't yield the fruit I might have hoped—two claimed they didn't know what I was talking about, and the third leveled every criticism I'd heard secondhand and more—the ministry director's observation made me examine my tendency to bolt at the first sign of trouble. Her wise words helped me discern that, unpleasant as the situation was, it was where the Lord wanted me.

The whispers never stopped. But two years later, my committee had delivered a redesigned, user-friendly website, the framework of which is still being used years later. One of the three critics has become a good friend.

To me, Giuseppina illustrates the call to trust big and to persevere despite what the world thinks of that trust and dependence on God. Giuseppina undoubtedly had dark moments. We all do when the going gets rough. (Mine generally come around 3:00 AM on weekdays.) Her life is an example that we can push away those self-doubts and live in total abandonment to him.

RADICAL THOUGHTS:

Here are a couple of verses to contemplate as you think about Giuseppina's life:

> "Are not two sparrows sold for a penny? Yet not one of them
> will fall to the ground unperceived by your Father…. So do

not be afraid; you are of more value than many sparrows."
(Matthew 10:29, 31)
"But he said to me, 'My grace is sufficient for you, for power
is made perfect in weakness.'" (2 Corinthians 12:9)

Consider journaling about the following questions, or use them to
spark discussion with a group of friends:

- Are you becoming impatient with the speed (or lack thereof)
  that something is progressing—a relationship, a weight reduc-
  tion program, a mortgage application—to the point that you're
  ready to give up? How do you know whether something is your
  plan or God's?

- How might you thank someone who serves or served as a valuable mentor to you on your spiritual journey for helping you
  persevere?

Praying with Giuseppina

St. Giuseppina, help me to be indifferent to the opinion of anyone
other than the Lord. Show me how to persevere in doing his will.

Resources

- View a video of Giuseppina's life.
- Learn more about the Daughters of St. Camillus.
- View a marvelous sculpture of Giuseppina and Father Tezza.

CHAPTER 4

Jacinta Marto
Willing to Sacrifice

The Basics
Born March 11, 1910, in Portugal | Died February 20, 1920, in Portugal
Canonized May 13, 2017 | Feast Day: February 20

Jacinta's Radical Gift
Having seen a vision of hell, St. Jacinta offered up lunches, persecution by those who doubted the children of Fátima, and other penances to keep others from suffering.

Jacinta's World
The year Jacinta was born, Portugal's monarchy was overthrown in a brief revolution. The successor Portuguese Republic, virulently anti-clerical, was called out in an encyclical by Pope Pius X for actions "breathing the most implacable hatred of the Catholic religion."[6] The 1918 influenza pandemic, which weakened the health of both Jacinta and her brother Francisco, is estimated to have cost at least fifty million lives worldwide.

Jacinta's Radical Path to Holiness
Lucia dos Santos would later describe her cousin Jacinta as a girl who liked to dance and had a good heart, but who was overly sensitive and liked to be in charge of their games. The two of them and Jacinta's older brother Francisco herded their families' sheep together, and Jacinta often could be found amid the animals. Lucia recalled that Jacinta once told her, "I want to do the same as Our Lord in that holy picture they gave me. He's just like this, right in the middle of them all, and he's holding one of them in his arms."[7]

It was some time later, on May 13, 1917, that the lady first appeared. Jacinta was seven, Lucia, ten, and Francisco just shy of his ninth birthday. The lady urged them to sacrifice so that souls might be saved, and she asked them to say the Rosary daily. She asked that they come back the thirteenth of each month.

The children initially agreed to keep the lady to themselves, but Jacinta couldn't resist telling her family, and soon the story spread. Still, they returned the next month. Then, the month after that, the lady showed them a vision of hell. That experience changed Jacinta profoundly. While all three made sacrifices to save souls from that fate, she was the leader in that regard—giving up lunches; wearing a rope around her waist; and withstanding pressure from relatives, clergy, and lay authorities alike to recant. By all accounts, Jacinta went from being a chatty, bossy girl to one given to introspection, even after the lady's final visit on October 13, 1917, which drew an estimated seventy thousand people. Through Lucia, the Blessed Mother urged the crowd to say the Rosary, repent of their sins, and make sacrifices.

Both Marto children and most of their family were struck by the flu epidemic in 1918, and Jacinta told Lucia the Blessed Mother had said that Francisco would go to heaven soon. When Mary asked if Jacinta was willing to convert more souls before her own death, the little girl said yes. Shortly before Francisco's death, Jacinta went to his side and asked him to tell the Lord and Mary that she was willing to suffer further.

Jacinta's final months were difficult. She had two ribs removed without being fully anesthetized. She was moved first to one hospital, then another. Three weeks before her tenth birthday, the girl who had spent a third of her life in the limelight was alone when she died.

In 1930 the Church recognized the apparitions as worthy of belief, clearing the way for public devotions to Our Lady of Fátima. Initially it was decided that Francisco and Jacinta could not be canonized because they were too young to understand or practice heroic virtues. But their cause was taken up again in 1979, and ultimately the Congregation for the Causes of Saints determined that in exceptionally rare cases, such gifts were possible. Jacinta and her brother were canonized on the one hundredth anniversary of the lady's first appearance.

Jacinta's Wisdom

"Our Lady…told us she would come and take Francisco to heaven, and she asked me if I still wanted to convert more sinners. I said I did."[8]

Living Radically Today

The hardest sacrifices can be the ones that seem the smallest, whether it's not eating delectable fruit, as in Jacinta's case, or watching the words that come out of our mouths.

The food sacrifices, I sort of got when I was Jacinta's age. During family grocery shopping on Saturdays, my sister and I could each pick out five candy bars for the week. One Lent, I gave up those candy bars. Then, on Easter morning before anyone else was awake, I crept downstairs and opened the box where they were stored, ready for sugar overload.

I took a bite out of the first one—it was stale. I took a bit out of the second one—stale. It was the same story with the third and fourth ones.

After that, I shied away from sacrificing up anything tangibly important for Lent, focusing more on the added service, prayer, and giving parts. Recently, however, I was brought up a bit short about a radical-and-hard-for-me-to-do sacrifice.

I go to dinner every six weeks or so with Laura and Rose. We catch up on our lives and talk about nerdy Catholic stuff. During the catch-up part, I started talking about all I had to do (including writing this book) and how I was making lists of my to-do lists. They both listened sympathetically, and then Rose asked what I regretted having said yes to. I think she was trying to help me establish practices for future boundary setting.

Rose looked shocked by my answer: "Not one thing."

We moved on, but I've thought a lot about that conversation. It's almost a professional sport where I live—people vying to see who's the busiest, the most overbooked, the most stressed. It may sound like a small sacrifice to you, but it's a big one to me. I'm working on opting out of that humblebrag. If I believe that my yeses are Spirit-led, then I also must trust that God will provide the time and the means for their fulfillment. I have stopped looking for the "atta-girl" and "I don't know how you do it all" validations that I had unconsciously been seeking. I am sacrificing that "venting" just as surely as Jacinta sacrificed her lunches and grapes, with the same hope that it will lead to the saving of souls, including this one.

Radical Thoughts

Here are a couple of verses to contemplate as you think about Jacinta's life:

> "Then Mary said, 'Here I am, the servant of the Lord; let be with me according to your word.'" (Luke 1:38)

> "And not only that, but we also boast in our sufferings,

knowing that suffering produces endurance...." (Romans 5:3)

Consider journaling about the following questions, or use them to spark discussion with a group of friends:

- What seemingly small sacrifice—tangible or intangible—are you avoiding? What would it take for you to embrace it?
- Identify a child, in your family or on the world stage, whose wisdom inspires you. How can you be more like that boy or girl?

Praying with Jacinta

St. Jacinta, I ask for your intercession to show me the way to avoid the fires of hell and to save as many souls as I can with my sacrifices.

Resources

- Check out the website for the Shrine of Fátima, which is visited in person by millions each year. The site offers live broadcasts for the Rosary, Masses, and more.
- Read Sister Lucia's memories of Jacinta, Francisco, and Fátima.
- Read an article by Brother John M. Samaha, SM, on the Fátima apparitions' historical context, published at the University of Dayton website.

CHAPTER 5

ELIZABETH OF THE TRINITY
Letting God Work with Our Frailties

THE BASICS
Born July 18, 1880, in France | Died November 9, 1906, in France
Canonized October 16, 2016 | Feast Day: November 8

ELIZABETH'S RADICAL GIFT
St. Elizabeth of the Trinity only lived to age twenty-six, which perhaps makes her compassion for her mother all the more radical. Elizabeth went from being a strong-willed child, given to tantrums, to a young woman who was patient with her mother's objections to her vocation. In Carmel, she was known as a thoughtful spiritual director and writer who inspired others by the way she embraced suffering.

ELIZABETH'S WORLD
To the outside world, France during Elizabeth's lifetime was experiencing a period of peace, prosperity, and innovation known as *La Belle Époque* (the Beautiful Epoch). More than thirty million people visited the 1889 World's Fair in Paris, which one entered through the Eiffel Tower. But it was also a time of strife for Catholics. A series of laws beginning in 1901 closed convents and confiscated Church properties. Religious men and women could no longer teach in schools. While Elizabeth's Carmelite convent in Dijon remained open, its chapel was closed to visitors.

ELIZABETH'S RADICAL PATH TO HOLINESS
The young Elizabeth was, shall we say, not given to self-control. One Christmas, when a favorite doll was used as the baby Jesus in

a church manger, the toddler loudly called out, "Bad priest! Bad priest!" and demanded the return of the doll. (To be fair, she also was seen teaching the doll to pray.) At least once, Elizabeth went into a room and kicked at the door until she regained her calm. Indeed, her outbursts were so severe that her exasperated mother once threatened to send her away to a nearby house of correction operated by nuns.

It's easy to understand why Elizabeth's mother, Marie Rolland Catez, might have been initially loath—or too distracted or tired—to exact much discipline. Marie, an only child, had lost a fiancé in the Franco-Prussian War (1870–1871). She was thirty-three when she married forty-seven-year-old Captain Joseph Catez; Elizabeth was born just ten months later after an exhausting thirty-six-hour labor. Less than three years later, a second daughter, Marguerite, was welcomed. The captain was away from time to time until his retirement in June 1885, and by then his health was failing. In 1887, the year Elizabeth turned seven, Marie lost her father and her husband, and moved with her two daughters to a home of more modest means in Dijon. The home happened to be less than a thousand feet from a Discalced Carmelite monastery.

It was about the same time that Elizabeth first whispered to a priest and family friend that she believed God desired her to be a nun. The prospect stunned her mother, who had already experienced so much loss. Marie hoped that this was a passing phase and made sure Elizabeth was involved in more earthly activities. The child became an excellent pianist, and she enjoyed outdoor outings with her sister and their friends.

People saw a marked change in Elizabeth's temperament when she made her First Communion in 1891. There were fewer and fewer public outbursts, more and more situations in which Elizabeth exercised patience and self-control. She would need every ounce of these, for ten years would pass before Marie would give her blessing for Elizabeth to enter the Dijon Carmel.

The same day as her First Communion, Elizabeth visited the Carmel parlor and met with the prioress, who would later say there had been something special about the girl even then. Despite a robust, joyous time full of friends and travel and pilgrimages, Elizabeth kept feeding her soul, with an eye toward religious life. She immersed herself in the writings of St. Teresa of Ávila (and in heading off Marie's plans for her to marry). When Elizabeth's confessor told Marie that he believed her daughter's vocation was real, Marie ordered her to stay away from Carmel. Elizabeth reluctantly obeyed.

Later, Elizabeth's sister, Marguerite, joined in urging Marie to embrace Elizabeth's vocation. Finally, Marie said she would acquiesce when Elizabeth turned twenty. By then, Elizabeth had read an early version of what would become Thérèse of Lisieux's *Story of a Soul,* which confirmed for her that she was called to become a Carmelite.

There was another delay in Marie's yes, however; she said that since neither Elizabeth nor the cleric who now served as their mutual confessor had discussed Elizabeth's vocation with her, she assumed the call had dissipated. Finally, two weeks after her twenty-first birthday, Elizabeth entered Carmel. She professed her vows on January 11, 1903.

In her letters from Carmel, Elizabeth continued to show compassion, love, and tenderness toward her mother despite Marie's years of stalling. While the first four months of her postulancy reflected a happy, contented state, her novitiate was marked by spiritual dryness, oversensitivity, and overdeveloped scrupulosity. She shared these concerns with two of her superiors, but never with her mother. Her letters to Marie were positive, cheerful, and upbeat, even as the end of Elizabeth's short life neared. In what is believed to be her final letter to Marie, written less than a month before her death from Addison's disease, Elizabeth wrote, "Oh, Mama, it is delightful, for He is there keeping me company, helping me to suffer, urging me to go beyond my suffering to rest in Him; do as I do, you will see how that transforms everything."[9]

At her beatification Mass in 1984, St. John Paul II noted that Elizabeth offered up both her physical and moral suffering "always assured of being loved and able to love. She gives in peace the gift of her wounded life."[10]

Elizabeth's Wisdom

"Receive every trial, every annoyance, every lack of courtesy in the light that springs from the Cross; that is how we please God, how we advance in the ways of love."[11]

Living Radically Today

We were having one of those big celebrations at my parish a while back. You know, the kind with dozens of tables; a line for the food; some music; and as is always the case at my parish, decorations that are way over the top and yet perfect at the same time.

My friend Kathy and I were standing back against the door, quietly taking it all in. Neither of us felt like being particularly social. That was when I noticed Faith. She's a member of a nearby parish, but she knows some folks at my parish from being on an Adoration team and in a charismatic prayer group. Faith was walking from table to table, smiling and greeting people, including total strangers. She also stopped at the perimeter chairs, where people were sitting by themselves, and even spent a few minutes with the unsociable-that-day Kathy and me. Sometimes, Faith got a nod or greeting in return; sometimes, people just looked at her. Their reactions didn't seem to matter; she listened when people wanted to talk (and some did, for several minutes); if they didn't, she smiled and kept moving. No one at the event could say they felt ignored or alone.

But it's not just in crowds that Faith's compassion shines. Three years ago, I stopped in at Adoration just before Thanksgiving Mass. I was not surprised to find one of my best friends there; I knew a physician had told her that week that her gravely ill husband was actively dying and needed to be moved to hospice. We caught each other's eye and stepped outside the chapel into the hallway and hugged, no words needed. Faith came in just then, chipper and full of holiday greetings. My friend said, "My husband's dying," and Faith enveloped us in a group hug and said a short prayer. She asked my friend for her husband's name and said she would offer up her hour for him, then went into the chapel and left us alone.

To my knowledge, Faith doesn't have to navigate the family boundary issues Elizabeth of the Trinity did; her mother is dead, and she's unmarried and childless. But to me, these two women are similar in that gift of carrying the Christ's comfort and joy to the world while still keeping focused on his desires. Faith could have stood in the back like Kathy and me, or she could have walked away feeling insulted the first time her greeting was ignored. She could have walked past my friend and me or insinuated herself further into what was obviously a deep personal moment. But she is wise and confident in the way she offers her radical compassion. She's active, not reactive, just as Elizabeth was in her relationship with her mother. She embraces Christ, not the world's dramas.

Radical Thoughts

Here are a couple of verses to contemplate as you think about Elizabeth's life:

"May you be made strong with all the strength that comes from his glorious power, and may you be prepared to endure everything with patience, while joyfully giving thanks to the Father, who has enabled you to share in the inheritance of the saints in the light" (Colossians 1:11-12).

"Self-control, then, is dominance over the desires" (4 Maccabees 1:31).

Consider journaling about the following questions, or use them to spark discussion with a group of friends:

- People who love us often want to hold us tight and keep us safe, especially when the Lord seems to be calling us in a direction they fear. How have you managed such situations, such as your choice of spouse, career, or location?

- What cross are you being called to pick up daily? How can you do it with less resentment and more joy?

Praying with Elizabeth

St. Elizabeth of the Trinity, help me to embrace the beauty and suffering that comes in obedience to God. Help me to be gentle with those who do not understand my vocation and seek to redirect me.

Resources

- The Carmelite Sisters of the Divine Heart of Jesus site includes a biography of St. Elizabeth and other canonized Carmelites.

- Watch a Boston College School of Theology and Ministry Continuing Education lecture on Elizabeth, part of a series on Carmelite authors.

- Not surprisingly, the Institute of Carmelite Studies has a robust catalog of Elizabeth's works. Consider reading her insightful letters from Carmel.

CHAPTER 6

TERESA OF CALCUTTA
Loving the Unlovable

THE BASICS

Born August 26, 1910, in North Macedonia | Died September 5, 1997, in India

Canonized September 4, 2016 | Feast Day: September 5

TERESA'S RADICAL GIFT

Mother Teresa was a radical truth speaker—whether it was delivering an anti-abortion lecture as part of her Nobel Peace Prize acceptance speech, telling the United Nations that holiness is not a luxury of the few, or replying, "Find your own Calcutta" to a high school student who wanted to know how to be like her.

TERESA'S WORLD

Teresa's homeland changed political hands as she grew up: from being part of the Ottoman Empire; ruled by the Serbs, then the Bulgarians; and eventually becoming part of what was known as the Kingdom of Serbs, Croats, and Slovenes. Calcutta in the years before Teresa moved there permanently experienced great unrest and suffering: a famine that claimed as much as 5 percent of the population; bombings during World War II; and the deaths of more than four thousand people in 1946 related to the desire for a Muslim state.

TERESA'S RADICAL PATH TO HOLINESS

You probably know the broad outlines of this story, since Mother Teresa was one of the most visible women religious—and perhaps one of the most visible women, period—of the twentieth century.

The youngest of three children, Anjezë Gonxha Bojaxhiu felt called to be a missionary from age twelve on. She discerned that she was to go to India, so she left for Ireland at age eighteen to become a Sister of Loreto. (The convent near Dublin was where missionary sisters learned English, the community's preferred language for those bound for India.) She chose her name in religious life for Thérèse of Lisieux; since another sister already had the name, she used the Spanish spelling. After just two months, Teresa left Ireland for India, arriving on January 6, 1929. In 1931, she was assigned to teach geography and catechism at the sisters' school.

Teresa seemed to be a natural teacher and administrator. Before her mid-thirties, she was principal of the school and overseeing a community of Indian women religious affiliated with the sisters. Then, two weeks after her thirty-sixth birthday, she was on a 400-mile train trip after a retreat when she received her "call within a call." The Lord wanted her to leave the convent to live among the poorest of the poor.

Twenty-seven months later, wearing the white-and-blue sari the world would come to know so well, Teresa experienced her first days in the Calcutta slums. The Society of the Missionaries of Charity was established less than two years later, and Teresa became an Indian citizen. The sisters ministered to those dying in the streets, to those suffering from a variety of diseases and disabilities, and to orphans. The year before she died, her community had more than five hundred missions in more than one hundred countries. All this happened as Teresa experienced a deep spiritual dryness that went on for decades.

The awards rolled in: the Nobel Peace Prize. An address to the United Nations. A speech to a National Prayer Breakfast in the United States. India's highest civilian honor.

There was just one thing: Teresa's propensity for speaking her truth, regardless of the audience, made many people uncomfortable.

It led them to look for inconsistencies in what she said and what she did, and it stirred up public criticism. She seemed to shrug it all off without a second thought—and kept talking.

Here are some examples:

- When she won the 1979 Nobel Peace Prize, she told the committee to help the poor with the nearly $200,000 that would have been used for a banquet. In her speech, she attacked abortion: "The greatest destroyer of peace today is the cry of the innocent unborn child. For if a mother can murder her own child in her womb, what is left for you and me to kill each other?"[12]

- Teresa also was radically blunt at a February 1994 National Prayer Breakfast, with President Clinton, Vice President Gore, and their wives in attendance: "Any country that accepts abortion is not teaching its people to love one another but to use any violence to get what they want."[13] She urged those considering abortion to "give the child to me."

- At the same event, she took on birth control other than natural planning: "In destroying the power of giving life or loving through contraception, a husband or wife is doing something to self. This turns the attention to self, and so it destroys the gift of love in him and her."[14]

- In a 1985 address to the United Nations, Teresa again called for an end to abortion and issued additional challenges to the delegates. Holiness, she told them, "is not a luxury of the few. It's a simple duty for each one of us." She also urged them to combat poverty in the very largest sense: "I find that the poverty of loneliness, the poverty of being unwanted, unloved…a throwaway of society, is a very difficult and very, very burdensome poverty, very difficult to remove."[15]

- In 1982, Teresa made a stop at a Catholic high school in northern Virginia, where a student asked her, "How do we become like you?" It almost certainly wasn't the first or last time she was asked that question. She didn't encourage the student to pray or do her homework or study Church teachings. "Find your own Calcutta," she said.

As I said, Teresa's truths may make you uncomfortable. There's no gray area there; to her, abortion, contraception, poverty, and the contemplation of the Lord's plan for a high schooler were all pretty cut and dried. She was radical in her straightforwardness, in the way she spoke truth. But then, so was Jesus.

Teresa's Wisdom

"Jesus died on the cross because that is what it took for him to do good to us, to save us from our selfishness and sin. He gave up everything to do the Father's will, to show us that we, too, must be willing to give up everything to do God's will, to love one another as he loves each one of us."[16]

Living Radically Today

So, what about that high school girl who asked Teresa how to be more like her? I met her twenty years later, after she'd attended a great university, earning degrees in commerce and information systems; gotten married; had three beautiful kids; and had a lovely home not far from where she'd grown up. At that point, Adrienne's Calcutta beyond her own family was co-facilitating a program for people like me who were away from the Catholic Church and were thinking about coming back. I warmed to her almost immediately; she could explain Church stances on hot-button issues with unapologetic insights, logic, and words that didn't condemn me and were easy to understand.

A few years later, her mom was diagnosed with leukemia. A number of Adrienne's friends had donated platelets. After a struggle, followed by a near-miraculous clearing of the cancer, followed by its relentless return, Adrienne's mom died, at peace and grateful for the gift of time she'd had with loved ones. My friend decided the best way to say thank you would be to donate platelets herself.

Except when Adrienne went to donate, her red blood cell count was so low, she wasn't accepted. The technician told her to have a few raisins before she came back to donate again. Adrienne mentioned this to her gynecologist at an appointment a few days later. Tests showed that at age forty, with no family history whatsoever, she had stage-three colon cancer. If her mom hadn't died and Adrienne hadn't decided to donate platelets, the cancer might have been discovered too late. Surgery and chemo followed almost immediately.

The treatment plan worked on Adrienne's body. But she was left with a dark night of the soul, struggling with what she was supposed to do with all this. A priest friend provided invaluable spiritual direction and then took her on a trip to Lourdes as a "Malade" with the Knights of Malta.

Slowly Adrienne felt her own "call within a call." She's now a board-certified chaplain, with a master's in pastoral theology. For this stage of her life, speaking the Lord's truth about illness and death to patients and families is her Calcutta. I'm sure she's doing it just as compassionately and warmly as she spoke the Church's truth to me. She's got a gift that way.

Radical Thoughts

Here are a couple of verses to contemplate as you think about Teresa's life:

"Then Jesus said to the Jews who had believed in him, 'If you continue in my word, you are truly my disciples; and you will know the truth, and the truth will make you free'" (John 8:31–32).

"This is the Spirit of truth, whom the world cannot receive, because it neither sees nor knows him. You know him, because he abides with you, and he will be in you" (John 14:17).

Consider journaling about the following questions, or use them to spark discussion with a group of friends:

- Which of Teresa's views makes you most uncomfortable and why?
- What is your Calcutta? What are you doing to ease the suffering there?

Praying with Teresa

St. Teresa, I tremble at the thought of saying aloud to an unreceptive audience the words the Lord places on my heart and soul. Help me to speak the truth, compassionately, but boldly.

Resources

- Franciscan Media has a number of other resources about Teresa, including *St. Teresa of Calcutta: Missionary, Mother, Mystic* and *Loving Jesus: Mother Teresa.*
- Check out the site for the Mother Teresa Center of the Missionaries of Charity to learn more about the saint's life and see videos and photos.
- Read the transcript of her 1979 Nobel Peace Prize acceptance speech.

CHAPTER 7

MARIA ELIZABETH HESSELBLAD
Standing for Inclusion

THE BASICS

Born June 4, 1870, in Sweden | Died April 24, 1957, in Italy
Canonized June 5, 2016 | Feast Day: June 4

MARIA ELIZABETH'S RADICAL GIFT

A Lutheran convert, St. Maria Elizabeth was radical in her efforts to unify all people in Christ, including the revitalization of St. Bridget's Order of the Most Holy Savior in Sweden and protection of at least twelve Jews at her Roman convent during World War II, which earned her Yad Vashem's Righteous Among All Nations award.

MARIA ELIZABETH'S WORLD

When Maria Elizabeth was born, Swedish citizens who practiced Catholicism could face exile or the death penalty. The law was changed in 1873, but it was not until the 1950s that Catholics were allowed to be teachers, nurses, or doctors. As a teenager, Maria Elizabeth was one of more than a million Swedes who immigrated to the United States between 1850 and 1910.

MARIA ELIZABETH'S RADICAL PATH TO HOLINESS

It's quite possible Elizabeth Hesselblad never knew a Catholic when she was growing up in a little town about 250 miles southwest of Stockholm. She, her parents, and her siblings (she was one of thirteen children, ten of whom survived to adulthood), like the vast majority of their countrymen and women at that time, were members of the Reformed Church of Sweden, a Lutheran denomination. The religious community that had been founded by Sweden's most famous Catholic—St. Bridget—had been expelled to Poland nearly three hundred years earlier, and citizens who practiced Catholicism did so at their own risk.

Living in late nineteenth century rural Sweden also brought risks of a different kind, and the Hesselblads moved several times, always looking for a better economic situation. Elizabeth left home at sixteen in hopes of finding a way to help support the family. Two years later, she ended up in the United States and began to study nursing.

It was while she was working in home nursing that Elizabeth had her first meaningful encounters with Catholics. While as a child she had wondered why there were so many different religions that prayed to the same God, she was taken aback by some of the practices of Catholics, especially invoking the name of the Blessed Virgin Mary in prayer.

Eventually Elizabeth went to work for a Catholic family, the Cisneroses. She grew so close to them that the family went to Sweden to meet the Hesselblads. Later, Elizabeth accompanied her employer to Europe, and at a Brussels cathedral, she experienced a conversion moment when she saw the Eucharist in a monstrance for the first time. In Rome, she was moved to pray when she saw the site, by then a Carmelite convent, where St. Bridget of Sweden had lived most of her last twenty years. Still, the time for Elizabeth's formal conversion was not ripe.

One of the Cisneros daughters entered the Visitation convent in Washington, D.C., and it likely was through that daughter that in 1902 Elizabeth met Fr. J.G. Hagen, a Jesuit priest who was director of the neighboring Georgetown University Observatory. She promptly asked him to receive her into the Church. When he demurred, saying they had just met, Elizabeth explained that she'd been struggling for years over the decision, and now was the time. The priest agreed to meet with her twice a day for three days, and he counseled her to spend the rest of those days in retreat. Three days later, on the Feast of the Assumption, she was received into the Church; two days after that, Elizabeth made her First Communion.

At the end of the year, a pilgrimage took Elizabeth to Rome, where she visited St. Bridget's residence. She felt called two years later to go back to Rome, and she looked into becoming a Carmelite. When ill health closed that door, she received a papal dispensation to become a sister of the Order of the Most Holy Savior, or Brigidines (also spelled Birgittines, Brigittines, or Bridgettines), even though few adherents remained.

Known as Maria Elizabeth in religious life, she spent the next few years visiting the community's remaining European convents, then reestablished the Roman community in 1911.

Maria Elizabeth also burned to bring the Brigidines back to Sweden in 1923, the 550th anniversary of St. Bridget's death, but convents still were not allowed in the country. Undeterred, she established a rest home operated by the sisters. Twelve years later, the Brigidines would open a convent in Vadstena, home of Bridget's first monastery, amid some local opposition. Sisters remain there today.

Meanwhile, the Brigidines were able to reestablish a convent in 1928 on the site of St. Bridget's Roman home. Maria Elizabeth would spend the rest of her life there, other than taking trips to visit communities abroad.

While Maria Elizabeth sought to convert souls to Catholicism, she had learned that inclusion and hospitality are the first steps to evangelization, covert or overt. Perhaps that's why she was sometimes able to overcome objections to the sisters' work and presence in Sweden. Further, her beliefs led her and two other sisters to hide at least twelve Roman Jews in their convent for about six months as the end of World War II approached. It has been estimated that more than a thousand Jews were deported from Rome to Auschwitz starting in early September 1943. After the war, the sisters were political agnostics, providing assistance to Germans, Italians, and Poles alike. Today, Brigidines in nearly twenty countries share the spirit of hospitality and ecumenical charity.

Maria Elizabeth's Wisdom

"The Lord has called us from different nations, but we must be united with one heart and one soul."[17]

Living Radically Today

It's comfortable to be around people who are just like us. A friend of mine once said that she was grateful she and her husband lived in a Catholic neighborhood, because that way, they knew the values (and parents) of their children's friends. My response was probably less than gracious; I noted that while I grew up in a very Catholic neighborhood, I washed a whole lot of cars and baked a whole lot of brownies for my friends in the Luther League and similar organizations for Episcopalians, Baptists, and Methodists, because the Catholic kids looked askance at me for going to public school.

But it does happen, that Catholic cocoon (or Lutheran, Episcopalian, Baptist, Methodist, Jewish, or Muslim, for that matter). And if we're supposed to go forth and proclaim the Good News, that's going to involve talking to people who aren't just like us, right in our own backyard.

Some might call Karla and her husband uber-Catholics. They're active in their parish and in a lay Catholic movement. They're involved in prayer groups and Bible study. They sent both their kids to Catholic high schools (one of them, by the way, to Visitation Preparatory, the same campus where St. Maria Elizabeth entered the Church). But Karla's Methodist grandmother was one of her key faith touchstones growing up. In fact, she still has her grandmother's Bible.

So it is perhaps fitting that for many years, Karla volunteered on Saturday mornings at a Methodist church near their home. They live in a vibrant, diverse community where dozens of languages are spoken, and Karla's fluency in Spanish was a valuable asset. For several hours each Saturday, Karla and other volunteers would provide support to people who were trying to figure out how to get jobs, how to navigate the process of bringing a relative to this country, how to get medical and other assistance, and in general, how to make life here work for them and their families. Some Saturdays, the line of people waiting to get in would wind around the block. And when they got inside, nobody asked if they were Methodist, Christian, or anything else. Karla and the other volunteers were there to be inclusive, to help them feel a part of the community and to show hospitality.

While that activity has ended, the church now provides a weekly breakfast for street people, where assistance with clothing and counseling also is available. And I'm betting those providing service still do so with a welcoming smile and handshake, not a closed door if the person in need happens to be of a different or no faith. They're not there to exclude. They're there to include—and reflect God's love radically.

Radical Thoughts

Here are a couple of verses to contemplate as you think about Maria Elizabeth's life:

"I ask not only on behalf of these, but also on behalf of those who will believe in me through their word, that they may all be one" (John 17:20–21).

"He answered, 'You shall love the Lord your God with all your heart, and with all your soul, and with all your strength, and with all your mind; and your neighbor as yourself'" (Luke 10:27).

Consider journaling about the following questions, or use them to spark discussion with a group of friends:

- When was the last time you got out of your "Catholic cocoon" and discussed faith with someone of another religion? Consider inviting a non-Catholic to coffee or a meal, not as an overt evangelization opportunity, but to learn more about the other person's beliefs and where they intersect with yours.

- Think about why you remain a Catholic, regardless of problems within the Church. Is it the Eucharist? Family tradition? Inertia?

Praying with Maria Elizabeth

St. Maria Elizabeth, open my eyes, my heart, and my arms to those who believe differently—and those who do not believe at all—so that I might love and serve as Jesus desires. May my words and actions always reflect him.

Resources

- The Abbey of Saint-Joseph de Clairval's July 23, 2001, newsletter has an extensive biography on the saint.

- The World Holocaust Remembrance Center, Yad Vashem, honored Mary Elizabeth and others as part of its education and research efforts. Learn more about the center's work.
- Learn more about the Brigidine Sisters and their presence in the world today.

CHAPTER 8

EUPHRASIA OF THE SACRED HEART
A Hidden Life of Prayer

THE BASICS

Born October 17, 1877, in India | Died August 29, 1952, in India
Canonized November 23, 2014 | Feast Day: August 30

EUPHRASIA'S RADICAL GIFT

During St. Euphrasia's lifetime, India went from a British colony to an independent nation, a time of disharmony and political activism. Through it all, the Praying Mother, as Euphrasia was known, was radical in her apostolate of prayer, forsaking leadership roles in her congregation for most of her life to pray for ten to twelve hours per day.

EUPHRASIA'S WORLD

England's Queen Victoria added "Empress of India" to her titles the year before Euphrasia was born. India's first presidential election was held on May 2, 1952, four months before Euphrasia's death. Mahatma Gandhi had been assassinated four years earlier, and one of his supporters, Rajendra Prasad, coasted to victory.

EUPHRASIA'S RADICAL PATH TO HOLINESS

As a child and even as a young woman, Rosa Eluvathingal was rarely healthy. This concerned her parents, wealthy landowners in southern India who were members of the Syro-Malabar Church, an Eastern Catholic Church. Rosa's younger sister had died as a child, and the parents worried that the same fate might befall their other daughter. Those worries led Rosa's mother to teach her to pray, especially the

Rosary, at a young age in hopes that divine intervention would protect her.

Perhaps it was that early, frequent communication with the Blessed Virgin that led to Rosa's vision of Mary at age nine. It was not long after that that she told her family she would never marry but instead would devote her life to Jesus. While a lucrative arranged marriage was more what her father had in mind for his only remaining daughter, after two years he relented and allowed Rosa to go to a Carmelite boarding school.

When she was nineteen, Rosa became a postulant with the Congregation of Mother of Carmel, a Syro-Malabar version of the Discalced Carmelites. She was given the name Euphrasia of the Sacred Heart for a fifth-century saint known for her piety and her resistance to temptations. Health issues plagued Euphrasia again, and the sisters considered dismissing her. But all her physical ailments miraculously disappeared after she had a vision of the Holy Family and was told she would live a good, long life as a nun. She made her perpetual profession on May 24, 1900, the day St. Mary's Convent in Ollur (about ten miles from her hometown) opened.

Euphrasia's early time as a woman religious followed the track of many. She was initially the assistant to the novice mistress, then the novice mistress. During that time, she was known as a bit of a disciplinarian who required her charges to resolve any disputes before they went to bed for the evening. (Mariam Thresia Chiramel Mankidiyan, who has a chapter earlier in this book, was one of Euphrasia's novices from November 1912 until January 1913. After Mariam Thresia left, she eventually established her own religious community.) Euphrasia then completed a three-year term as mother superior. But in 1916, for whatever reason, she left the leadership track—and her focus on prayer intensified.

As early as 1904, Euphrasia wrote a detailed practice for praying with different legions of angels, starting at four in the morning and not concluding until very late in the evening. This was not theoretical to Euphrasia. When anger and worry—challenges that carried over from her childhood—threatened, she prayed. When she was tempted, she prayed. When her rheumatism or other health problems troubled her, she prayed. To express her devotion to the Blessed Sacrament and Mary, she prayed. Small wonder, then, that within the convent, she became known as Evuprasiamma, the praying mother. Her sisters would find her at prayer for ten to twelve hours a day, sitting in the chapel (she couldn't kneel for that long) and sometimes holding a sixteen-inch crucifix.

While Teresa of Calcutta was ministering to the street people of Calcutta 1,400 miles away, Euphrasia was praying. It's pretty radical when you think about it, that for decades Euphrasia devoted so many hours to conversing with the Lord. Perhaps that's why the little girl who was so sickly lived to age seventy-four—fifty-two of them spent as the praying nun.

Euphrasia's Wisdom
"My joy is in leading a hidden life unknown to others."[18]

Living Radically Today
I met Diane when she was the assistant director at a weeklong Christian writers conference and I was one of the instructors. I was a bit uneasy about this; I had only said yes because a colleague who had planned to go ended up with a conflict. In addition, I had a family reunion the following week in the same state, and the conference center was on a lake. Beyond that, I knew a fair amount about writing, but squat about Christians, since I'd stopped going to Mass

more than twenty years earlier. I didn't know if they'd condemn me, speak in tongues, try to convert me, or what.

So, when everything went wrong the day I arrived—from the director not arranging for me to be on the shuttle from the airport sixty miles away to my room being under someone else's name to getting lost on the way to the dining hall—I was less than understanding at dinner. (Plus, I was starved, not having had anything to eat for fourteen hours.) I screeched at Diane about all these problems and calmly, one by one, she addressed my concerns: She'd make sure I had a ride back to the airport at the end of the week. She'd show me how to get to my room. She'd carry my tray, if I wanted. It was frustrating, not having anything left to be angry about. I sort of hated her for that.

The next morning, I got up just before sunrise to go to the lakefront and sort out my thoughts and gird myself for the day, which would include a sort of tent revival gathering. When I got to the lake, Diane was already there, sitting on a bench. We nodded at each other and she moved down a bit to allow plenty of room between us.

Neither of us said a word for the next fifteen minutes as the sun slowly climbed. Then, *wham!* It broke the horizon, shooting rays all across the water. I gasped at the beauty.

Diane turned toward me. "It's something, isn't it?"

"Yes! I love sunrises, but I don't know the last time I saw one on the water. Maybe never."

She nodded. "This is a thin place."

I gulped. "What is a thin place?"

"One where it's easier to get to God."

We sat there, silently, for another fifteen minutes or so until the dining room opened for breakfast. We didn't really talk about it, but each morning for the rest of the week, we watched the sunrise together. My anxiety lessened each day; no one spoke in tongues or tried to convert me or asked me much of anything about my faith life or lack thereof. Diane and I had a lot of serious talks and giggly moments with other writers.

She and I both went back to the conference for four or five years; then things changed. It got scaled back, and people who lived closer were hired to run it and teach at it. We both moved. We now live two hundred miles apart and are in touch only sporadically, mainly because I get busy. My most fruitful prayer time remains sunrise, though. I can't pray for half a day as Euphrasia could, but even fifteen minutes of silence each day helps keep me on course.

Last summer, Diane and I were back at the conference center for the first time in a dozen years. We both were at the lakefront before sunrise. And as the rays shot across the water, I realized anew just how radical the power of prayer and quiet are, so much more so than tent revivals and come-to-Jesus witnesses. They can spark revolutions—and conversions.

RADICAL THOUGHTS
Here are a couple of verses to contemplate as you think about Euphrasia's life:

"Do not adorn yourself outwardly by braiding your hair, and by wearing gold ornaments or fine clothing; rather, let your adornment be the inner self with the lasting beauty of a gentle and quiet spirit, which is very precious in God's sight" (1 Peter 3:3–4).

"Set your minds on things that are above, not on things that are on earth, for you have died, and your life is hidden with

Christ in God. When Christ who is your life is revealed, then you also will be revealed with him in glory" (Colossians 3:2-4).

Consider journaling about the following questions, or use them to spark discussion with a group of friends:

- Do you have a favorite place to pray—a comfy chair, an Adoration chapel, in front of beautiful scenery (or a picture thereof)? Can you commit to spending just fifteen minutes today in that place?

- Mix up your prayer style. For example, if you're a Rosary person, try the Divine Mercy Chaplet. If you use the adoration-contrition-thanksgiving-supplication model, consider focusing on a different letter each time you pray, rather than attempting to cover all four.

PRAYING WITH EUPHRASIA

St. Euphrasia, your life is a true illustration of the importance of setting my schedule around prayer, not the other way around. Please pray for me, that I might emulate your example.

Resources

- The St. Euphrasia Pilgrim Centre site features a lengthy biography of the Praying Mother as well as a video from her canonization.

- View her canonization Mass.

- The Congregation of the Mother of Carmel site includes a biography and much information about the community's activities today.

CHAPTER 9

Laura Montoya Upegui
Shrugging Off Others' Judgment

The Basics
Born May 26, 1874, in Colombia | Died October 21, 1949, in Colombia
Canonized May 12, 2013 | Feast Day: October 21

Laura's Radical Gift
After a difficult early life, St. Laura taught school and thought about becoming a cloistered nun. Instead, in her forties, Laura was radical in embracing Colombia's indigenous people whom many regarded as "beasts" and beyond redemption.

Laura's World
Colombia saw repeated internal strife throughout Laura's life. The Panama Canal opened on August 15, 1914. Her father died in the 1876 Colombian Civil War; the Thousand Days' War occurred from October 1899 to November 1902; and a ten-year civil war called *La Violencia* began the year before her death.

Laura's Radical Path to Holiness
Wars have serious ripple effects on people beyond those who fight them, and Laura's family was an example of this. The middle of three children, two-year-old Laura's life changed drastically when her father was killed in a civil war. The child was sent to live first with her grandmother, then to an orphanage managed by an aunt who was a nun. Sixteen-year-old Laura had had little formal education herself when she was sent to Medellín to be trained as a schoolteacher to help support the family.

Her certificate in hand, Laura proved to be a talented high school teacher. By the time she was twenty-three, she had become a school's deputy director. But in her soul, she was feeling called to religious life. She dreamed of becoming a Discalced Carmelite.

In the meantime, Laura began doing volunteer work among the indigenous people, including Colombians of African descent, north of Medellín. Struck by the communities' needs, she established Works of Indians, a charitable organization to provide support. Her efforts often met with disdain and disbelief: Why did Laura think this was work appropriate for a woman, and why was she concerning herself with a population many considered to be "wild beasts"? But Laura ignored such criticism, and she slowly came to discern that her calling was as an active woman religious, not living in a cloister.

At age forty, Laura founded the Congregation of the Missionary Sisters of Immaculate Mary and St. Catherine of Siena with the local archbishop's support. She and a handful of other women—by some accounts including her mother, Dolores—ventured to Dabeiba to begin missionary work in earnest.

Now, Dabeiba is only about 110 miles northwest of Medellín. But it was a different world. Medellín had about seventy thousand residents and was growing rapidly. It's called the "City of Eternal Spring" because its climate is so lovely all year round. Dabeiba's average temperature is 78 degrees (compared with Medellín's 72.5 degrees); the average annual rainfall in Dabeiba is 124 inches, 80 percent more than in Medellín.

Riding mules and horses through the jungle, it took the women nine days to get to Dabeiba. Once there, they engaged the residents using what Laura called the "pedagogy of love," teaching people about Jesus Christ by getting to know them and offering friendship, rather than simply reciting Church dogma and doctrine.

Laura spent more than thirty years in the jungle, despite the disapproval of many in "proper" Christian society. The price of her ministry was her health; she spent her final nine years in a wheelchair at the Medellín motherhouse. Today, the sisters continue her work in twenty-one countries in the Americas, Africa, and Europe.

At the first Colombian-born saint's canonization, Pope Francis said that she "teaches us to accept everyone without prejudice, without discrimination, and without reticence, but rather with sincere love, giving them the very best of ourselves…"[19]

Laura's Wisdom

"He needed bold, brave, inflamed women in the love of God, who could assimilate his life to that of the poor inhabitants of the jungle, to raise them to God."[20]

Living Radically Today

Offering mercy and assistance to people or entities familiar to us and our life experience seems to come naturally. For me, that includes families struggling to find a place to live, supplies for school kids, Catholic media outlets.

I hope I wouldn't have been among those who criticized Laura for her ministry, groundbreaking as it was at the time, and probably you hope the same about yourself. But I'm pretty sure I couldn't have lived in the jungle, away from running water and electricity. In the same way, I am in awe of my friend Jean's ministry that I know I'm not cut out for: prison outreach. The thought of that door clanging and being on the same side with convicted felons with no easy way to get out makes me, ahem, uncomfortable.

Jean spent years being on teams for the Kairos ministry at a maximum-security prison for women about a two-hour drive from her home. It's a serious commitment of time; in addition to the three-and-a-half days of talks, discussions, and the like, there are requirements for team members to follow up as a group. She and others I've known in prison ministry say one key thing they've learned is that they could have been on the other side of the bars except for the grace of God and a good support system in difficult times.

Jean's background surely helped her prepare for this work. She was a parish director of religious education and a pastoral counselor for nearly three decades, as well as being a trained spiritual director. She also served in the Ignatian Volunteer Corps for many years.

She continues to minister to five women who were formerly incarcerated and are dealing with the difficulty of finding jobs, reuniting with their families, and struggling with substance abuse. One woman spent weeks living with Jean until she found housing.

In addition, Jean is engaged in perhaps the most challenging prison ministry of all: supporting a longtime friend who has been incarcerated for a crime no one who knows him believes he committed. Jean writes him often, and she is among those who have visited him. Regardless of whatever might come to light down the road, good or bad, about the accusation against this man, I know Jean will continue to be his friend, just as St. Laura was to those some considered subhuman.

RADICAL THOUGHTS

Here are a couple of verses to contemplate as you think about Laura's life:

> "You are righteous, O Lord, and all your deeds are just; all your ways are mercy and truth; you judge the world" (Tobit 3:2).

"Do not now be stiff-necked as your ancestors were, but yield yourselves to the Lord and come to his sanctuary, which he has sanctified forever, and serve the Lord your God, so that his fierce anger may turn away from you" (2 Chronicles 30:8).

Consider journaling about the following questions, or use them to spark discussion with a group of friends:

- Do you know of someone suspected or convicted of a heinous crime—murder, perhaps, or sexual abuse—that you don't believe is worthy of mercy? How can you unharden your heart enough to pray for this person?
- Consider using St. Laura's pedagogy of love to bring Christ to a friend or family member who is away for the Church. How would you do that?

Praying with Laura

St. Laura, help embrace the world as you did. Help me to put aside the prejudices I've amassed and to see with Christ's eyes those I struggle to embrace as brothers and sisters.

Resources

- The website for her community is rich with photos, videos, and other information about this saint and the work that the Missionaries of Mary Immaculate and St. Catherine of Siena do today.
- The Archdiocese of Medellín site features a painting of Laura late in life and a brief biography.
- The Colombian president's office has produced a three-hour video of Laura's canonization. It's in Spanish, but take a look even if you don't understand the language. The video features a number of images of the saint at various ages.

CHAPTER 10

Anna Schäffer
Turning Pain into Praise

The Basics

Born February 18, 1882, in Germany | Died October 5, 1925, in Germany

Canonized October 21, 2012 | Feast Day: October 5

Anna's Radical Gift

Anna Schäffer wanted to be a missionary. Falling into a boiling laundry vat took away any possibility of that happening; she was bedridden for the rest of her life. After an internal struggle, she had a radical realization: Missionary work didn't have to involve getting on a train or ship—it could be done right from her bed.

Anna's World

The Neuschwanstein Castle (the inspiration for Disneyland's Sleeping Beauty Castle), about seventy miles from Anna's home in Mindelstetten, was completed when she was four. Bavaria, the region in which she lived, had become part of the German Empire in 1871 but remained a monarchy until the end of World War I. About eighteen months after her death, Karl Ratzinger, Pope Emeritus Benedict XVI, was born in Marktl, about eighty miles southeast of Mindelstetten.

Anna's Radical Path to Holiness

From a young age, Anna knew she was meant to be a missionary. There was just one problem: money. She was the third of six children, and income had never come easily to the family. With minimal schooling, Anna went to work as a housekeeper when she was just thirteen. The family's financial situation became even more precarious when her father died in January 1896. But Anna was a hard worker, and she knew if she kept working hard, she could save the funds she needed for a dowry, join a convent, and realize her dream.

In June 1898, Anna had a vision that troubled her greatly. She saw Jesus as the good shepherd holding a rosary, and she heard him say that she would suffer greatly before her twentieth birthday. Anna was so concerned about the vision that she left the place she had been working and found another job.

Just two weeks before her nineteenth birthday, it was laundry day. A stovepipe above the laundry kettle at her employer's establishment had become loose, so Anna climbed up on the rim of the kettle to fix it. Instead, she fell into the boiling water. A coworker was so frightened that he ran for help rather than thinking to first get her out of the kettle. Those lost precious minutes proved crucial.

Three months in the hospital failed to provide much healing for Anna, nor did two lengthy stays in a university clinic. Her wounds remained open. The treatments shock us today—for example, her foot joints were broken in hopes of improving her mobility. More than thirty surgeries were performed. Nothing worked. There was little to be done other than send her home to Mindelstetten to be cared for by her mother. Anna would never walk again.

It didn't seem right, and it didn't seem fair. Hadn't God put on Anna's heart that she had a calling as a missionary? For two years, she struggled to see the purpose in this tragedy. With time, she adjusted her thinking, and she began to see her disability as a cross to be picked up and carried daily.

Anna said she had three tools with which to bring souls to the Lord: her suffering, her needle, and her penholder. With her needle, she did embroidery, sewing, and knitting for others, including churches and chapels. With her pen, she kept journals about her suffering and responded to letters and prayer requests. She also listened to the stories of those who came to visit her. Anna came to realize that she was indeed a missionary, just in a different way than she had expected.

During her years of pain, Anna received Communion nearly daily, and she also received the gift of stigmata, which she took care to hide.

In April 1923 she was diagnosed with colon cancer; a month before she died, she lost the ability to speak. Her radical example of adjusting her God-given vocation to meet her life circumstances is an example to all of us who question why things happen that seem to take us off course. Anna shows us that where there's a vocation, there's a way—even if we're bedridden.

Anna's Wisdom

"How easy it is to die with Jesus on the cross—if one has lived with Jesus on the cross!"[21]

Living Radically Today

Molly was just three when she started singing with the choir at her Lutheran church. Yes, she was—and still is—that good. When you hear her killing those high notes, it's easy to imagine her in a heavenly choir taking on solos and receiving applause from the Almighty himself. It was obvious to all that Molly was going to do something, really do something, with that voice.

But as she entered her teens, Molly started having problems with her eyesight. The diagnosis was retinitis pigmentosa, a rare genetic visual disorder. Neither of her parents suffer from it. What happens is that the cells in the retina, the lining of the eye, break down and stop working. Eventually, many people with retinitis pigmentosa become completely blind.

Molly doesn't talk much about when she received the diagnosis and prognosis at thirteen, but I'm betting there was at least a brief dark night of the soul. How would she use her God-given gift of a beautiful voice if she couldn't see?

It would have been easy to give up and become bitter. But instead, Molly adjusted. She earned master's degrees in theological studies and counseling. When the time came, she welcomed Mileigh, her wonderful guide dog, into her life.

About five years ago, Molly and a friend she'd met at work camp years earlier realized they both wanted to be more than friends. She converted to Catholicism, moved hundreds of miles from her family and support system, and married Philip in 2016. Their first daughter was born in December 2017; a second followed in late 2019, along with the heartbreak of a twin to that second daughter dying during Molly's pregnancy.

Molly sings to Philip and their babies. She's a cantor at her parish; Mileigh leads her to the ambo. And she's part of an auditioned choir that performs about a half-dozen times per year throughout the Washington, D.C., area.

Retinitis pigmentosa didn't end Molly's ministry; it just adjusted it, like Anna Schäffer and her fall into that kettle. From the two of them, I learn to radically embrace adjustments in my own life, confident in the Lord's direction and love.

Radical Thoughts

Here are a couple of verses to contemplate as you think about Anna's life:

"I tell you, my friends, do not fear those who kill the body, and after that can do nothing more" (Luke 12:4).

"The prayers of faith will save the sick, and the Lord will raise them up; and anyone who has committed sins will be forgiven. Therefore confess your sins to one another, and pray for one another, so that you may be healed" (James 5:16).

Consider journaling about these questions, or use them to spark discussion with a group of friends:

- Are you holding on to an injustice or hurt, closing off a corner of your soul to the Lord? How might you adjust your outlook?

- We all can be tempted to envy a friend or acquaintance who seems to have the perfect life. But we never know anyone else's full story of struggle. How can you move closer to an appreciation of the person's gifts and away from begrudging what he or she seems to have?

Praying with Anna

St. Anna, help me to embrace the adjustments the world puts in my path but to never veer off the course the Father desires.

Resources

- The Church of Mindelstetten, Germany, hosts a site devoted to the saint, including pilgrimage information.

- Check out the Diocese of Regensburg, Germany, video *Anna Schäffer: Life and Meaning of a Saint*. While the audio is in German, the images are definitely worth a look.

- Some of Anna's notes have been collected into a book, *Thoughts and Memories of My Life, of Illness and My Longing for the Eternal Homeland*. The entries are short and inspiring.

CHAPTER 11

MARIANNE COPE
Providing Care With Courage

THE BASICS

Born January 23, 1838, in Germany | Died August 9, 1918 in Hawaii (now the United States)

Canonized October 21, 2012 | Feast Day: January 23

MARIANNE'S RADICAL GIFT

Marianne Cope listened only to God, accepting and caring for people others feared or found distasteful and putting her own health at risk.

Marianne's World

When she was two, Maria Anna Barbara Koob (the name *Cope* was adopted later) moved with her family from Germany to Utica, New York. Utica's population had exploded from about three thousand to nearly thirteen thousand in twenty years. Industrial development helped to attract immigrants. The city also was an important stop on the Underground Railroad for those escaping enslavement in the South. In the years after she arrived in Hawaii, the islands experienced revolution, abdication of the final queen, establishment of a republic, and then annexation to the United States.

MARIANNE'S RADICAL PATH TO HOLINESS

Fr. Leonor Fouesnel, who was assigned to Hawaii's Catholic mission, sent a letter to more than fifty communities of women religious. It identified the need for sisters to run hospitals and schools and to "procure the salvation of souls and promote the glory of God and the interest of our holy religion…"[22]

But every community declined. Every community, that is, until the letter made its way to Mother Marianne Cope, provincial superior for the Sisters of St. Francis in Syracuse, New York. She felt called and wrote back for more information. Future letters from Fr. Leonor talked about the islands' climate; the salary the sisters would receive; and the possibility Protestants would be asked to help if the Sisters of St. Francis didn't say yes. A month would pass before, during a personal visit to the sisters, Fr. Leonor disclosed that the work would be among those who suffered from Hansen's disease, in those days called leprosy.

Hansen's disease struck fear in the hearts of most people. It was believed—later disproved—that the infection that strikes the skin, nervous system, and more was highly contagious. When the infection went untreated, those with the disease often were crippled, paralyzed, and blinded. As a result, in Hawaii and elsewhere, those suffering from Hansen's disease and sometimes their family members were cast out from society. And based on the information available at the time, anyone working with those stricken put his or her health at severe risk.

Knowing all this, the community's vote was radical in its courage: eight to one in favor of going to Hawaii. Within a few months, Mother Marianne and five others were on their way.

Hard work and criticism were nothing new to Mother Marianne. After she finished school, she had worked at a factory, possibly the textile mill across the street from her parents' home. Her plan upon beginning her novitiate in 1862 was to be a teacher, and while she did that for a time, her focus changed to healthcare and administration. She helped to establish central New York's first two Catholic hospitals, where she was reproached for allowing alcoholics and other undesirables to receive treatment. What she and the others found when they arrived in Hawaii was much more challenging: The facility she was to manage had been built for one hundred people but housed double that. Conditions were deplorable. But instead of turning around and leaving on the next boat, Mother Marianne and the others chose to stay.

Mother Marianne became a tireless advocate for those she served. When she learned patients were being abused at a hospital near Honolulu, she gave an ultimatum: Either the administrator left, or the sisters would. She won control of the hospital. The sisters also set up a home within the hospital campus to tend to the daughters of those with Hansen's disease, for no other facility would care for the girls, and they took on responsibility for additional hospitals and schools.

Mother Marianne and Fr. Damien, known as the apostle to the lepers, met after she had been in Hawaii only a few months. When he himself was diagnosed with Hansen's two years later, she courageously nursed him and took on his work among men with the infection.

Despite thirty-five years in ministry on the islands, Mother Marianne never contracted the disease. Her insistence on strict sanitary and hygiene procedures generally are credited for this. She died of natural causes in 1918. Her remains currently reside at the Cathedral Basilica of Our Lady of Peace in Honolulu.

Marianne's Wisdom

"Let us make best use of the fleeting moments. They will not return."[23]

Living Radically Today

You don't have to have a physical disease to feel like an outcast. Sometimes it happens when you don't look or speak like other people. Maybe you're new to the country or the area; maybe you dress differently from others.

Or maybe, you just run into mean girls.

I had a new position in a new city. There was a lot of turnover due to uncertainty about the company's future. During the transition, my predecessor shared that Miranda, who was on an extended maternity leave, had asked for still more time, and the company's leadership had decided against it. Communicating the decision was left to me. Let's just say the conversation didn't go well. Miranda chose not to come back.

Two years later, I left for a nonsupervisory position with a more stable business. Someone mentioned at a going-away party that, thanks to a college friend, Miranda had just started with the same company.

When I walked in the following Monday, it was obvious my new colleagues had heard Miranda's side of the story. There were no welcoming chit-chats with anyone who wasn't a supervisor, no offering to show me the ropes, no invitations to lunch. People turned away from me in the hall, in the bathroom, in staff meetings. Miranda in particular was given to whispering whenever she saw me.

The one exception was Teresa. She'd started the same day as me in a similar position. While she hit it off with the others, she still treated me like a human being. We bounced work stuff off one another, and we were known to have a beer or two together after our weekly late night at work. I never mentioned Miranda, and neither did she.

After about a month, the deep freeze started to thaw—I think primarily because Teresa vouched for me. After another month, Miranda started treating me civilly; we never discussed what had happened at the last job. Four months later, she quit to return to the freelance writing world and a more family-flexible schedule.

I stayed at that job for nearly nine years. Some of the women eventually became good friends with whom I'm still occasionally in touch. My main takeaway from that time is how Teresa consistently rose above the fray, radically treating the cool kids, the weirdos, and everyone else—from the janitors and security guards to the company owners—with the same kindness and respect.

Both Marianne Cope and Teresa show me that everyone, no matter how vile we might privately think they look or act, is deserving of that radical acceptance and respect. After all, God gives it to them… and to us. Even the smallest kindness we provide can give them hope that they can be made clean.

Radical Thoughts

Here are a couple of verses to contemplate as you think about Marianne's life:

> "I hereby command you: Be strong and courageous; do not
> be frightened or dismayed, for the Lord your God is with
> you wherever you go" (Joshua 1:9).

> "But God will not take away a life; he will devise plans so as
> not to keep an outcast banished forever from his presence"
> (2 Samuel 14:14).

Consider journaling about these questions, or use them to spark discussion with a group of friends:

- Where are you avoiding sharing even the basics of Christian love with someone simply because he or she is different from you? Perhaps it's a homeless person you see at the bus stop, or someone at work or in your neighborhood who is of a different ethnicity or speaks a different language. How might Mother

Marianne's example inform your next interaction with that person?

- Think about a situation where you feel like an outcast. Ask a priest or spiritual adviser for thoughts on how to embrace the Lord's love for you and shed your worries about worldly rejection.

PRAYING WITH MARIANNE

St. Marianne, help me to find the courage and vision to see Christ in all those I encounter, regardless of my initial reaction to their differentness.

RESOURCES

- The St. Marianne Cope Museum in Syracuse, New York, includes audio-visual exhibits, images, and artifacts of the saint.
- Check out the video that the Sisters of St. Francis of the Neumann Communities put together when Marianne's canonization was announced.
- The Cathedral Basilica of Our Lady of Peace in Honolulu, where the saint's remains now reside, features biographies and photos of her and St. Damien of Molokai.

CHAPTER 12

MARY MACKILLOP
Pursuing God's Plan Despite Roadblocks

THE BASICS

Born January 15, 1842, in Australia | Died August 8, 1909, in Australia

Canonized October 17, 2010 | Feast Day: August 8

MARY'S RADICAL GIFT

Mary MacKillop was excommunicated for insubordination, and later she was told to move her congregation out of a diocese. Through it all, she showed a radical trust in God and the Church, even when some of its leaders were less than Christlike.

MARY'S WORLD

When Mary was born, Australia consisted of six colonies with a total population of around three hundred thousand. While gold had been found earlier on the continent, discoveries in 1861 in New South Wales and Victoria prompted large population influxes, bringing the number of Australians to more than four million by the end of Mary's life. On January 1, 1901, the colonies formed the Australian Commonwealth.

MARY'S RADICAL PATH TO HOLINESS

Faith and trust in God were about the only things that ever seemed to come easily to this daughter of Scots immigrants to Australia, who would be known as Mary of the Cross in religious life. One of the many things that always came hard was money, and so the MacKillop children—Mary was the oldest of eight, seven of whom lived past their first birthday—periodically were farmed out to other relatives. When she was sixteen, Mary went to work at a Melbourne stationery store, and with her brother John, she took on most of the financial responsibility for the family.

Two years later, Mary moved to the private town of Penola to serve as a governess to some of her cousins; an aunt and uncle had been the area's first European settlers and had done quite well for themselves compared with the MacKillops' hardscrabble existence.

It was in Penola that Mary met Fr. Julian Tenison Woods, who was under pressure from his bishop to provide a Catholic education for area children. He became Mary's spiritual director, and the two talked about establishing a community of women religious. However, in the meantime, Mary had taken a teaching position about a hundred miles away, and her family had joined her there. Growing more desperate after a couple laywomen he had hired for the school both left, Fr. Woods again reached out to Mary. While she felt she couldn't leave her family since she was their main financial support, a younger sister agreed to fill in. Classes were held in the local church until Mary's brother John managed to fix up an unused stable.

In 1866, Mary returned to Penola. By later that year, she, one of her sisters, and some companions began forming a religious community with Fr. Woods's help. He was moved up the coast nearly 250 miles to Adelaide a year later, where he faced the same educational challenges. Mary and the others agreed to join him. Fr. Woods wrote the Sisters of St. Joseph community's rule, and Bishop Laurence Sheil approved it in late 1868. Within a year, the "Brown Joeys," as they were known because of their habits, were in charge of nearly two dozen schools, a women's shelter, and an orphanage.

But trouble was ahead. Mary and three other sisters moved to Queensland at the invitation of Brisbane's bishop. Severe disagreements ensued over control of the schools—Mary believed it belonged with the sisters; the bishop, with the diocese. Mary returned to Adelaide in April 1871 to more headaches. Rumors were starting to bubble up about sisters' teaching abilities, as well about Fr. Woods's behavior. Indeed, almost soon as Mary had arrived, he sent her off to visit the society's residences throughout the region.

During Mary's travels, she became aware that some community members had told Fr. Woods that they were hearing allegations of sexual abuse by a priest. After an investigation, the accused priest was ordered to leave Australia. Another priest then promised revenge. His complaints about the sisters and his view that they needed to be under diocesan control found their way to Bishop Sheil, the same bishop who had approved the community's original rule.

Back in Adelaide, on September 22, 1871, after receiving a letter from Mary stating her desire to continue to operate the community according to that rule, Bishop Sheil excommunicated her and evicted the sisters from their residence. On his deathbed the following March, the bishop ordered her excommunication rescinded.

Concerns about all the Adelaide turmoil resulted in an apostolic commission investigation. While Mary was exonerated, Fr. Woods was removed as the society's director and reassigned seven hundred miles away.

Intent on moving the community beyond diocesan politics, Mary left Adelaide in March 1873 and did not return until January 1875. When she met with Pope Pius IX in Rome, her first stop, he called her "the excommunicated one." After traveling throughout Europe, Mary was called back to Rome and accepted a revised constitution.

Back home in Australia, Mary continued to encounter opposition from the bishops, who believed they needed more control over the sisters. This round of discord included the bishop of Adelaide, who in November 1883 sent Mary to Sidney. It is perhaps not surprising that Mary was removed as superior general in favor of a more pliable sister. Mary served as her assistant superior general, but the pair failed to see eye to eye on many topics. To add to Mary's challenges, Fr. Woods died in 1889; their relationship had never been completely repaired.

When the superior general died, the sisters returned Mary to that role, a position she would hold until her death. A stroke in 1902 confined her to a wheelchair but had no other effects on her abilities. Indeed, she was elected to another term as superior general three years later.

Mary's Wisdom

"Whatever troubles may be before you, accept them cheerfully, remembering whom you are trying to follow. Do not be afraid."[24]

Living Radically Today

Paula is one of the most fearless people I know. Not that she's a skydiver or bungee jumper or anything like that; it's that she doesn't hesitate to intervene on behalf of and advocate for people whose voices can get drowned out.

An elderly woman who I knew slightly and admired greatly was a good friend of Paula's. One day, the two of them were together, and someone who didn't identify himself as a reporter started asking the older woman questions. Her politically charged comment went viral and spelled the end of her career. At some professional risk, Paula wrote an essay providing some much-needed context to what had happened and the importance of journalists being transparent about conducting interviews.

Outside of work, Paula spent years taking on her public school system to get her son the help he needed. By the time he was in middle school, it was apparent he was a different sort of learner, having trouble focusing on teachers and on homework. He was diagnosed with ADHD. As the disconnection deepened, Paula and her husband navigated a new world that included individual education programs, medication, even the recommendation that their son be hospitalized. It was discouraging at times for Paula, having experts attempt to manage her expectations about what her son could do in the right learning environment.

Finally, after five years, things started to fall into place, starting with a diagnosis of a sleeping disorder. Paula's investigation of resources led the family to a program where hands-on learners' needs were understood and addressed. Today, her son is an adult with his own successful business. He's happy.

The story doesn't end there. For Paula, it wasn't enough that she and her husband found the right path for their son. She believes all children have the right to programs that help them feel intelligent and valued. She hosts a radio show on education innovation and has written a book about the family's journey.

I didn't know Paula while she and her husband were navigating all this, but when she talks and writes about the path now, she is calm and positive, not castigating teachers and other professionals who might have been more helpful. I asked her recently how she does that. Her quick response was her faith; she always trusted that God was with her and would guide their family.

Paula never gave up on her son, any more than Mary MacKillop gave up when she was excommunicated and later ordered to move her community out of a particular diocese. They share a radical, confident faith that the Lord has set them on a particular path. Both Mary and Paula remind us that when we truly surrender to God, we surrender, or at least try to, our hopes of being popular and well-liked by everyone. People are going to misunderstand, question, and judge what we do. That is not our concern. He provides us with all we need to do his work, and he, not others or earthly setbacks, will determine our success.

RADICAL THOUGHTS

Here are a couple of verses to contemplate as you think about Mary's life:

> "For surely I know the plans I have for you, says the Lord, plans for your welfare and not for harm, to give you a future with hope" (Jeremiah 29:11).

> "Therefore, my beloved, be steadfast, immovable, always excelling in the work of the Lord, because you know that in the Lord your labor is not in vain" (1 Corinthians 15:58).

Consider journaling about these questions, or use them to spark discussion with a group of friends:

- Mary had difficult relationships with a number of priests during her life, but she always remained calm and cordial, trusting that God knew the truth. How can her example help you navigate a troublesome time with a priest, family member, or friend?

- Compromise is often the right course of action, but not at the cost of sacrificing our core values and beliefs. What are the non-negotiables for you, and how do you explain your position to those who don't agree with you?

PRAYING WITH MARY

St. Mary, help me to put aside my temptation to let my desire to be one of the "cool kids" when it conflicts with faithful obedience.

Help me to trust and to believe that being popular with God is all that matters.

RESOURCES

- The Sisters of Saint Joseph of the Sacred Heart site features information about both the saint and Father Julian Tension Woods—and is rich in details about the work that goes on today.
- Take a tour of Mary MacKillop Place in North Sidney. MMP includes a chapel with the saint's tomb, a museum, gift shop, and more.
- Visit the site for the Mary MacKillop Penola Centre, where the saint and Father Julian Tenison Woods began their work in 1866.

CHAPTER 13

ALPHONSA MUTTATHUPADATHU
Coping with Pain

THE BASICS
Born August 19, 1910, in India | Died July 28, 1946, in India
Canonized October 12, 2008 | Feast Day: July 28

ALPHONSA'S RADICAL GIFT
Alphonsa Muttathupadathu spent thirty-six years on the earth, most of them in pain of one sort or another. Yet this Franciscan Clarist remained physically active, radically offering up her suffering as an oblation.

ALPHONSA'S WORLD
India's first woman saint lived in the country's southern tip in what is now the state of Kerala, where tradition holds that St. Thomas founded churches and evangelized. Unlike the well-traveled Thomas, it appears that Alphonsa spent her entire life there. Kerala is the same region where two other radical saints, Mariam Thresia Chiramel Mankidiyan and Euphrasia of the Sacred Heart, lived. Today, more than half Kerala's 34 million residents identify as Hindu; Catholics represent about 11 percent.

ALPHONSA'S RADICAL PATH TO HOLINESS
Named Anna Muttathupadathu, she was the youngest of five children born to a respected, though not particularly wealthy, doctor and his wife who were members of the local Syro-Malabar Catholic Church. The pain in Anna's life would begin before she was even old enough to sit up. Anna's mother died when the baby was just three months old, and Anna was sent to live with her grandparents.

They provided Anna with a loving home and an example of Christian faith. They nursed her through a year-long bout with eczema when she was just three, and it's said that by the time Anna was five, she could lead the family's evening prayers.

When Anna was ten, her late mother's sister took over her care. Her aunt was an exacting sort, intolerant of any action or word she interpreted as disobedience or rebellion. Her main goal, it seems, was to see her niece married off. Since Anna was a beauty, finding suitors was not a problem for the aunt despite the girl's lack of a dowry.

During this challenging time, Anna had a vision of St. Thérèse of Lisieux, to whom she had a special devotion since Thérèse's mother had died before Thérèse was four. In the vision, Thérèse told Anna that she too would become a saint.

At thirteen, Anna felt that she was out of options in pursuing her true vocation to be a bride of Christ. While some say it was an accident that she severely burned one of her feet in an ash pit, Anna's own words indicate it was intentional. Regardless, the incident left her in pain and partially disabled for the rest of her life. It also seems to have dissuaded her aunt from finding Anna a husband. During her suffering after this incident, Anna said she was visited by Kuriakose Elias Chavara, a Kerala priest who had died in 1871 (and who was canonized in 2014).

One of Anna's uncles was a priest and chaplain to a Franciscan Clarist convent less than twenty miles away, and he encouraged her to pursue her vocation there. She entered on Pentecost 1927, and she found the community's discipline less taxing than living up to her aunt's expectations had been. In religious life, she would be known as Alphonsa of the Immaculate Conception. When her health permitted—and often, including when she suffered a severe wound on her leg, it did not—she served as a primary school teacher while preparing herself for religious life.

In December 1936, four months after professing her final vows, Alphonsa experienced what appeared to be a miraculous cure from all her ailments. She credited the intervention of Father Chavara; she said he told her in a vision that, while her existing issues would not recur, she would face more suffering. Indeed, that proved to be the case. In 1939, pneumonia weakened her considerably; the following year, she suffered what may have been a form of post-traumatic stress amnesia after a thief entered her cell. In September 1941, she received last rites due to a painful abscess; however, she again recovered, this time thanking St. Thérèse of Lisieux.

The final year of Alphonsa's life was marked by more recurrent medical issues, including vomiting, convulsions, and chills and fever. Those who knew her said she never complained about her myriad ailments, keeping a smile on her face at all times. At her beatification, St. John Paul II's homily reflected those witnesses:

> She constantly accepted all her sufferings with serenity and trust in God, being firmly convinced that they would purify her motives, help her to overcome all selfishness, and unite her more closely with her beloved divine Spouse.[25]

Alphonsa's Wisdom

"I am prepared to suffer more. I know the Lord is with me. He has some plan for me. How can I requite his kindness?"[26]

Living Radically Today

Maura is an extremely private person; we were friends for ten years before I had any idea of her age. She looks at least fifteen years younger than she is, perhaps because of her serene nature and joyful smile.

That's especially remarkable given the amount of physical trauma she has experienced in the past thirty-plus years. Her car was rear-ended, resulting in Maura experiencing chronic back and neck pain. Another time, the car she was riding in was rear-ended, and the collision resulted in a separated shoulder that kept her confined to bed. She was forced to quit her job, and legal efforts to get the responsible party to help with her medical expenses failed, so she never had the recommended surgery.

A few years later, Maura was again behind the wheel when her car was T-boned as she was arriving for a prayer gathering at some friends' house. This time, the impact was on her left side, reinjuring the left side of her neck, separating her left shoulder, and filling her mouth with glass.

A couple of years ago, Maura was walking up the outside stairs at a friend's home when a branch caught her purse and pulled her backward down the steps. The back of her head slammed on the concrete, and she spent a few days in the hospital with a severe concussion. Months passed before she recovered enough to drive at night. Yet almost immediately, she was able to joke that while she may have cracked her head, she managed to save the bottle of wine she was carrying.

Maura lives on her IRA, Social Security, and the occasional dog sitting gig. She doesn't invite people into her townhouse because she says she can't keep it up as she would like due to her physical condition. It would be understandable if she focused on all the pain and misery, physical and otherwise, life has brought her. But she doesn't; I know about some of them only by chance, not because she talks much about how she's hurting. Those discussions, I suspect, she has with her guardian angel, whom she credits to saving her life more than once, and Padre Pio, to whom she has a special devotion.

Rather, she picks up her cross and follows Jesus. She spent several years helping grieving families arrange funeral Masses and receptions. She attends a weekly prayer group. The times I've needed someone to help people feel welcome at events, Maura has been the first person I've turned to. That smile is heartfelt, inviting, and contagious.

We all have days with physical, emotional, or spiritual aches and pains, days when we just want to pull the covers over our heads and surrender to a pity party. Maura and St. Alphonsa remind us that there's a whole world out there waiting for our Spirit-inspired smile.

Radical Thoughts

Here are a couple of verses to contemplate as you think about Alphonsa's life:

"As for me, I am already being poured out as a libation, and the time of my departure has come. I have fought the good fight, I have finished the race, I have kept the faith" (2 Timothy 4:5–7).

"As they left the council, they rejoiced that they were considered worthy to suffer dishonor for the sake of the name" (Acts 5:41).

Consider journaling about these questions, or use them to spark discussion with a group of friends:

- Do you have a chronic condition or temporary ache or pain that causes you to withdraw from time with family and friends? Without causing further injury to yourself, how might you offer a bit of suffering up to be present to others?
- We all have friends who seem to have dark clouds over their heads. (Another of my friends had a house fire, a broken hand,

and a basement sewage backup all in less than a year.) Consider spending time listening to the person's tale of misfortune and praying for him or her rather than giving the person sure-fire remedies to solve everything that's going wrong.

PRAYING WITH ALPHONSA

St. Alphonsa, my suffering is nothing like yours, let alone what our Lord endured. May I keep trust in the Father in front of me.

RESOURCES

- The St. Alphonsa Pilgrim Centre site includes much information about the saint's life and the museum dedicated to her, along sections of images and prayer requests.
- The Syro-Malabar Church site provides a detailed timeline of Alphonsa's life along with a photo gallery and videos.
- Learn more about the Franciscan Clarist Congregation and the work members do today.

CHAPTER 14

GIANNA BERETTA MOLLA
Trusting God No Matter What

THE BASICS

Born October 4, 1922, in Italy | Died April 28, 1962, in Italy

Canonized May 16, 2004 | Feast Day: April 28

GIANNA'S RADICAL GIFT

Gianna Molla was a physician who loved her husband and children. She fully understood the risks of a problem pregnancy. Gianna was radical in refusing any procedures that would injure the baby, even if that would put her own life at increased risk.

GIANNA'S WORLD

Benito Mussolini became Italy's prime minister the month Gianna was born. She and other women gained the right to vote when the Italian republic was established after World War II. Catholics and others were scandalized by Italian director Federico Fellini's 1960 satire *La Dolce Vita*, but that didn't seem to suppress the film's success at the box office around the world.

GIANNA'S RADICAL PATH TO HOLINESS

It took Gianna a while—a good long while by some standards—to discern her true vocation.

She was the tenth of thirteen children born near Milan to loving parents who set an excellent example of faith; both were secular Franciscans. A flu pandemic in Italy was at its worst in 1918–1920, ultimately resulting in an estimated 466,000 deaths there. In the next few years, more died, including some of Gianna's siblings. The family moved first to Milan's hill country, then to Genoa, then back to the Milan area. The reasons were myriad: the World War II bombings of Genoa, the desire to be closer to family, and the search for a healthier climate. Indeed, when Gianna herself was in her late teens, her health was poor enough that she had to suspend her studies for a year. It was around that time that she went on a spiritual retreat and prayed that the Lord might make his will known to her.

The year Gianna turned twenty brought seismic change: Her parents died within four months of each other. Two of her brothers entered seminaries. Gianna determined she would begin studying medicine, just as one of her seminarian brothers had. While in school and living with her paternal grandparents, she became active in the St. Vincent de Paul Society and Catholic Action. By all accounts, she enjoyed life, with plenty of friends, vacations, and other activities we would consider typical of a young woman in her twenties today.

In 1949, having received degrees in surgery and medicine, Gianna contemplated joining her missionary brother and physician, now known as Brother Alberto, in Brazil. The prospect appealed to her greatly, but after much discernment, she was advised against pursuing the idea due to her own uncertain health. Instead, the following summer, she opened her own clinic and gained certification in pediatrics. The clinic happened to be across the street from where Pietro Molla's parents lived.

Pietro, ten years her senior, later recalled noticing Gianna as she was giving his sister a transfusion around the time Gianna opened her clinic. They had another chance encounter when he had a doctor's appointment with one of her brothers. It was not until 1954, when they were attending a mutual friend's first Mass, that they first conversed. Within a year, they were married, and in November 1956, they welcomed their first child, a son. Two daughters followed quickly thereafter, then the heartbreak of two miscarriages. They were a happy family, despite Pietro's business travel, including a trip to the United States. In addition to her family, her burgeoning medical practice (which now included medical director of maternity and daycare centers and pro-bono work as a school physician), and continuing service to Catholic Action, Gianna found joy in opera, fashion, dancing, skiing, and other sports. She and Pietro wrote each other often while he was away.

When Gianna became pregnant again, she and Pietro agreed that she would stay home with the children after the baby's birth. But at two months, Gianna was found to have a non-cancerous uterine tumor. The experts gave her three options: complete hysterectomy to remove the growth, which would also result in the baby's death; removing the growth and terminating the pregnancy; or simply removing the tumor and continuing the pregnancy, knowing that complications could occur in the next seven months.

The first option would have been the lowest risk to her—and apparently would not have been a Church issue because it would have truly been aimed at saving Gianna's life. The second would have meant the possibility of more pregnancies, but at the cost of the baby. Gianna, who as a physician had a keen awareness of the risks related with all three options, chose the third.

Seven months later, a healthy baby girl was born; they named her Gianna Emanuela. But a week later, Gianna herself was dead of an abdominal wall infection that spread into her bloodstream. Today, with prompt medical care, she likely would have lived. Gianna Emanuela went on to become a physician herself, and she was at her mother's canonization along with her father and her two surviving siblings.

Turning over control to God often is difficult, and it can be especially challenging when our expertise and knowledge of the situation make the surrender more complicated, as was the case with Gianna Beretta Molla. And yet, she did not hesitate in her radical trust, selecting the best course for her unborn child, even though it brought increased risk to herself.

Gianna was among a group of six people who in 2004 would become the last saints canonized by St. John Paul II. His description of her shows an understanding of that radical selflessness: "The extreme sacrifice she sealed with her life testifies that only those who have the courage to give of themselves totally to God and to others are able to fulfill themselves."[27]

Gianna's Wisdom

"Our earthly and eternal happiness depend on following our vocation without faltering."[28]

Living Radically Today

Kallie always loved children. She knew she'd be a great mom. And so, when the time came to marry the man she loved, she was over the moon with joy. She knew he would be a good husband and father.

Except it didn't happen that way.

For reasons that aren't important here, the marriage ended hastily and was quickly annulled. In the meantime, Kallie pursued teaching. That special gift of connecting with children could be used in the classroom until God presented her with her true life companion.

Kallie kept teaching. She moved. She dated, but nothing serious developed. She wondered if she was being too picky. She decided she wasn't. Then, a man began stalking her. The police said they could do nothing to help her. She moved again, this time nearly a thousand miles away.

A decade later, Kallie is still single. She owns a townhouse with her brother, and their parents live down the street. And each and every day, she puts on her spiritual armor and goes into a public school classroom. It's a tough, confusing time to be a middle schooler; the boys and girls don't always get much help with homework, manners, or any rules at all at home. When they enter Kallie's classroom, they often don't understand why it's important to turn in reports on time or be kind to other children or be respectful to adults. Some of her colleagues don't think it's worth the risk of pushback from parents and administrators to hold the students accountable. Kallie has taught long enough that she understands the risks—and she accepts them because she knows the kids are worth it.

I'm sure she has moments she wishes life had worked out the way she initially dreamed, with a houseful of kids and a loving husband. But after discernment, Kallie has embraced living her maternity vocation in this way with all her heart and soul. Maybe that's why, year after year, her former students, including some of those who were the most challenging initially, come back to thank her.

Radical Thoughts

Here are a couple of verses to contemplate as you think about Gianna's life:

> "Trust in the Lord with all your heart, and do not rely on your own insight" (Proverbs 3:5).

> "And so observe, from generation to generation, that none of those who put their trust in him will lack strength" (1 Maccabees 2:61).

Consider journaling about these questions, or use them to spark discussion with a group of friends:

- Identify an issue you're struggling with because as much as you love God, all the world and your worldly knowledge tell you to go in a different direction than he desires. What would help to quiet your soul, even if the expert comments aren't going to go away?

- Gianna thought she was called to be a missionary, and she had to have been disappointed initially. Then she discerned she could provide the same healing services as a mother, physician, and volunteer. Do you have a tugging at your heart to return to a dream from childhood or young adulthood? What could you do to incorporate it in your life today?

Praying with Gianna

St. Gianna, help me to surrender my own analysis of risks and benefits so that I may say yes with a loving heart and soul to what the Father asks.

Resources

- Gianna was a patron saint of the 2015 World Family Meeting in Philadelphia, which was attended by Pope Francis. Take a look at a Salt and Light Media video produced at that time, featuring numerous images of Gianna and her family.

- The Society of St. Gianna Beretta Molla site features a robust look at the saint's life and information about the St. Gianna Shrine in Pennsylvania.

- Gianna Emanuela Molla shares in a LifeSiteNews video interview what she learned from her father, and how her mother's example inspired her.

CHAPTER 15

MARIA DE LAS MARAVILLAS DE JESÚS
Fearlessly Pursuing Her Vocation

THE BASICS
Born November 4, 1891, in Spain | Died December 11, 1974, in Spain
Canonized May 4, 2003 | Feast Day: December 11

MARIA MARAVILLAS'S RADICAL GIFT
After Vatican II, some religious communities thought they needed to update the way their vocations were lived out. Maria Maravillas didn't have a problem with that—as long as she could be in a community that lived in the manner of Teresa of Ávila's Discalced Carmelite reforms. She was radical in her recognition that change without discernment often isn't wise.

MARIA MARAVILLAS' WORLD
Spain was a monarchy during Maravillas' childhood and her early years in the convent. With the establishment of the Second Spanish Republic in 1931, Catholicism came under attack, with laws that restricted Church property ownership and Church-related public events. During Spanish Civil War (1936–1939), it's estimated that the Republicans killed more than 6,800 clergy and religious and an untold number of Catholic laypeople. While the Church hierarchy supported Francisco Franco and the Nationalists during the conflict, Franco's repressive policies later caused a shift in Catholic support. Franco died the year after Maravillas.

MARIA MARAVILLAS' RADICAL PATH TO HOLINESS
It was as simple as this: From an early age, Maria Maravillas burned with the desire to be a Carmelite. And nothing—not her mother,

not a civil war, not even Vatican II—was going to stand in her way of living her vocation in the manner in which Teresa of Ávila had reformed Carmel in the sixteenth century.

At times, however, that proved to be far from simple.

She was the fourth child born to a prestigious, devout Madrid family. When Maria de las Maravillas ("Wonders") Pidal y Chico de Guzmán was born, her father was Spain's ambassador to the Holy See. She grew up hearing her grandmother's stories of the lives of the saints and, inspired by St. Agnes, offered a vow of chastity at a very early age. When she was old enough to read herself, the works of Teresa of Ávila and John of the Cross resonated so deeply with her that she discerned a vocation as a Discalced Carmelite, living a life of prayer and contemplation in a cloistered community.

When Maria Maravillas was nineteen, her father died, followed soon thereafter by her beloved grandmother. It's understandable why her mother was initially reluctant to "lose" her daughter as well. Finally, in 1919, a few weeks before her twenty-eighth birthday, Maria Maravillas entered a Carmelite convent about thirty miles from her home.

That same year, Spain's King Alfonso XIII erected a monument to the Sacred Heart of Jesus not far from Madrid at the country's geographic center. Maria Maravillas had barely made her first vows when she and another sister felt called to establish a monastery near the site. In May 1924, the Cerro de los Angeles (Hill of the Angels) convent was opened by Maria Maravillas and three sisters; she took her final vows there the same month and was named prioress in 1926, a role she would hold for forty-eight years. Another convent, this one in India, followed in 1933.

Simmering social and political unrest in Spain boiled over into civil war on July 17, 1936. The sisters at Cerro de los Angeles had already been threatened by militants once, and just five days after the war began, were ordered to leave the monastery. Fortunately, an Ursuline convent nearby welcomed them until they were able to find an apartment. They spent fourteen months there, under close watch. As the war raged on, Mother Maravillas's community left Madrid and, after spending twenty-four hours in Lourdes, was able to found a new convent in northern Spain in 1937. When the war ended in April 1939, the sisters returned to Cerro de los Angeles to find the monument in ruins and the convent in not much better condition. That, however, did not stop them from living there as they rebuilt; after all, they were happy to be home again.

The next several decades under Mother Maravillas's leadership saw rapid expansion, with eight more Spanish communities established. Madrid's La Aldehuela community, which opened in 1961, would be Mother Maravillas's home until her death. She likely took special joy in a 1964 request to restore the first community in which she had lived, and then to revitalize Ávila's Incarnation monastery, where St. Teresa had lived for nearly forty years.

St. Teresa, you may recall, embarked on a reformation of the Carmelites in the sixteenth century, taking them back to their roots of poverty, enclosure, and prayer. It was the model Maravillas fully embraced, right down to requiring the use of stockings and sandals as close to St. Teresa's as possible. She brushed aside any suggestions to relieve the austerity of the convents and their cells, saying in essence that the Discalced Carmelites would go on even if those convents didn't. Mother Maravillas followed a plan of austerity herself, reportedly only sleeping three hours a night, while sitting upright on the floor. She did all this while living through her own dark night of the soul.

Two significant events occurred in the fall of 1962: Mother Maravillas had her first heart attack, and the Second Vatican Council opened. When it closed in December 1965, among the provisions was that leaders of religious communities would revise their governing documents, working with all related monasteries, and send the documents for approval by the Holy See. Since the Discalced Carmelite monasteries are autonomous, that proved a challenge, and to Mother Maravillas's point of view, it would move them away from their roots.

In 1972, Mother Maravillas had her second heart attack, but she also won a victory in her struggle to keep her monastic family as she believed it should be. She received approval for the Association of St. Teresa, an organization of monasteries that remained under existing governing practices. When she died two years later, Mother Maravillas expressed her happiness to leave the world as a Carmelite.

MARIA MARAVILLAS'S WISDOM

"Whatever God wants, as God wills, when God wills."[29]

LIVING RADICALLY TODAY

From an early age, my friend Grace knew her vocation would be as a wife and mother. What she didn't know was how long it would take her to get there.

Grace came to the Washington, D.C., area for college and did all the things young women do in D.C.: She got a contracting job with top-secret clearance, made a lot of money, and worked a lot of hours. She signed a lease on a nice apartment. She found her way back to regular Mass attendance, and in a Catholic young adults' group, she met a great guy who accepted her obsessions with *The Godfather, The Sound of Music,* and Bruce Springsteen. She switched to a government job with predictable hours. She and the great guy got married, and after some difficulty, Grace got pregnant. She prepared for stay-at-home mom-dom.

Check, check, check—kind of like Maravillas's life before the Spanish Civil War. But at this point, Grace's life took a heartbreaking turn. Due to a botched delivery, her full-term baby son died before either she or her husband could ever cuddle with him. His room, decorated with such love and joy, was empty. Grace and her husband were warned that it would be very difficult for her to ever become pregnant again.

Except—she did.

A year later, they welcomed their sweet daughter. A couple years later, a son arrived.

Grace and her husband bought the home of their dreams. It has plenty of room for the kids to run around, and it's less than two blocks from their parish and the parish school. Grace walks their daughter to preschool every day and is involved in school committees. It's easy for her husband to take the subway to work.

A few months after they moved in, Grace gave me the grand tour of the house. "It's exactly what you've always wanted!" I gushed.

Grace smiled. "It is," she said. "I just never would have imagined how long, or how hard, it would be to get here." Then one of the kids did something cute, and we both started laughing.

Like Mother Maravillas, Grace wasn't afraid to pursue her vocation, regardless of the barriers she faced. With faith—and in her case, bolstered by her husband and excellent medical care—she climbed over each one. That's what radical women do.

RADICAL THOUGHTS

Here are a couple of verses to contemplate as you think about Maravillas's life:

"The wisdom of the humble lifts their heads high, and seats them among the great" (Sirach 11:1).

"My faithfulness and steadfast love shall be with him; and in my name his horn shall be exalted" (Psalm 89:24).

Consider journaling about these questions, or use them to spark discussion with a group of friends:

- Is there something that small, still voice inside you is asking you to do, but the world is advising you against it? Maybe it's taking on a challenging ministry or having another child. Sketch out what your life would look like if you said yes.

- When the going gets tough, we can be tempted to give up. What resources might help you renew your resolve to staying on the path the Lord desires for you?

PRAYING WITH MARIA MARAVILLAS

St. Maravillas, sometimes I get so discouraged. Everyone else's life seems easier than mine. Please help me to accept the Lord's plan rather than let it be drowned out by those who think I'm behind the times or naïve.

Resources

- The Abbey of Saint-Joseph de Clairval's October 18, 2000, newsletter has an extensive biography on the saint.

- Read the Teresian Carmel General Curia's biography of Maravillas, and learn more about the community today.

- Venezuela's Academia Hagiografía has put together a short video about the saint's canonization and her life, with photos from all ages. Even if you don't speak Spanish, you'll find it of interest.

CHAPTER 16

GENOVEVA TORRES MORALES
Sacrificing Solitude for the Needs of Others

THE BASICS

Born January 3, 1870, in Spain | Died January 5, 1956, in Spain
Canonized May 4, 2003 | Feast Day: January 5

GENOVEVA'S RADICAL GIFT

St. Genoveva was on crutches nearly all her life. One might think that she would live out her vocation in the solitude she became inured to as a child, and indeed, she would have liked to have become a Carmelite Sister of Charity had she been considered healthy enough. But she wasn't, and so instead she was led down the path of establishing a religious community that provided support for destitute elderly women. She radically accepted her frequent pain and offered it up in service.

GENOVEVA'S WORLD

When Genoveva was born, Spain was in the midst of a six-year revolt that ended with the brief establishment of the First Spanish Republic. The country returned to monarchy from 1886 to 1931. The Second Spanish Republic—regarded as extremely anti-clerical, expelling the Jesuits and banning monks and nuns from teaching in schools—followed for five years. After the Spanish Civil War, the country was under Francisco Franco's dictatorship for the rest of Genoveva's life.

GENOVEVA'S RADICAL PATH TO HOLINESS

Loneliness and pain were two things Genoveva knew well, really well. Both of her parents and four of her five siblings died by the time she was eight. She went to live with her only remaining immediate family relative, an older brother named José. He was not abusive to her, but he was a man of few words, with little empathy. Genoveva focused on her household chores. There was no time for friends, no time for play, no time for school, no time for much of anything other than work. She did, however, spend enough time in parish catechesis to make her First Communion and be confirmed.

When Genoveva was thirteen, a tumor formed in her left knee and, perhaps because of a lack of early medical attention, gangrene developed. In a crude operation on the family's kitchen table with inadequate anesthetic, part of Genoveva's leg was amputated. She would never again walk without crutches.

The following year, Genoveva took a bad fall, and her injuries were such that José and his new wife did not believe they could handle her care. They sent her to the Carmelite Sisters of Charity's facility in nearby Valencia, where she spent the next nine years, one of about seven hundred residents.

It's easy to understand why Genoveva would have felt accepted among the sisters and staff in Valencia. The community was founded by Joaquina Vedruna de Mas (canonized in 1959), who died about fifteen years before Genoveva's birth. Joaquina, a mother of nine, had herself suffered physically; she had attacks of internal bleeding in the final five years of her life and also experienced progressive paralysis. In addition, Genoveva received spiritual direction from the home's chaplain, Fr. Carlos Ferris, who a few years later would cofound a home for those suffering from Hansen's disease, then known as leprosy. Father Ferris encouraged her to explore a vocation with the Carmelites of Charity.

However, Genoveva's own health was deemed to be too poor for acceptance into the community, so in 1895, she returned to her hometown. There, she and two housemates cobbled together lives that included prayer and just about enough money to get by themselves and to help elderly single women who were even worse off than they were. At times, homeless women were invited to live with them, and Genoveva began to think there should be a community of women religious to focus on helping women in this situation. Because of her own desire for solitude and physical ailments, it probably seemed unlikely to her that she would be involved in the creation, let alone the leadership, of such an effort.

Seventeen years later, in 1911, Genoveva, with the assistance of Church authorities, established the first community of what would be known as the Sacred Heart of Jesus and the Holy Angels, nicknamed the Angelicas. Six more homes followed quickly across Spain. Diocesan approval came in 1925, and Genoveva was elected and reelected again and again as superior general. This left her with less time than she would have liked for time alone with God, and the activities that leading a community require taxed her physically. The woman known as "the angel of solitude" shouldered those sufferings—and said yes to the Lord's plan for her.

Amid the fears and dangers of the Spanish Civil War, the Angelicas' homes provided safe havens for poverty-stricken women and other laypeople as well as, on occasion, other women religious. The community received final formal approval in 1953.

By then, Genoveva's health issues had worsened. She lost much of her hearing. She resigned as mother general in 1954, and at Christmas in 1955, suffered a stroke. She died the following January.

Genoveva's Wisdom

"Even if I must suffer greatly, thanks be to God's mercy, I will not lack courage."[30]

Living Radically Today

I love editing.

I'm not talking about proofreading or even copyediting. Believe me, I understand the value of correct spelling, grammar, and punctuation. (A special thank you here to the Franciscan Media team, who most likely have removed several thousand extraneous commas by this point in this book.) But they are not my gifts.

The editing I love is working with writers to help their material resonate with readers. It's a delicate, nuanced process; the end product, whether it's a novel, memoir, how-to book, essay, or technical manual, still needs to sound like *they* wrote it.

Freelance editing kept food on the table and the lights on in the three or so years it took me to repay more than a hundred thousand dollars in bankruptcy debt, a time when my take-home pay from my day job was less than a thousand dollars a month. It's a time I remember fondly for many reasons: I relearned how to live simply. I met a lot of cool people who are still friends today. And I came back to the Church.

For years, my friend Patricia nagged me to write, saying writers have way more fun than editors. As I was walking home from Mass on December 25, 2005—having received the Eucharist for the first time in thirty-three years at my first-ever Christmas Day Mass—I started thinking about all the people who had helped me return to my faith, including Patricia. I remembered what she'd always said about writers needing to unzip their souls and expose their foibles— and boy oh boy, did I have foibles to expose. So I wrote a memoir, which didn't get published for reasons that I won't go into here. But one thing led to another, and several books for Catholic publishers later, here I am.

Writing still doesn't come as easily to me as editing, and I suspect Genoveva's care and feeding of the Angelicas never came as easily to her as her time in solitude. I suspect there were days she would have preferred spending time in Adoration or reading Scripture to going over the bills or meeting with young women exploring a vocation. But I'll bet she loved those public times as well, because they provided her with unexpected blessings, and she knew in her soul that it was where God wanted her at that particular moment.

I believe that about Genoveva because it happens to me. My friend Meg once said she envisioned the women saints chatting in a heavenly parlor, saying, "Whom shall we send to talk with Mel today?" And on those days when I'd rather be editing, working on genealogy, or doing just about anything other than writing, someone like Genoveva starts whispering her story in my ear to share with you. For me, it doesn't get any better than that.

RADICAL THOUGHTS

Here are a couple of verses to contemplate as you think about Genoveva's life:

"Now there are varieties of gifts, but the same Spirit; and there are varieties of services, but the same Lord; and there are varieties of activities, but it is the same God who activates all of them in everyone" (1 Corinthians 12:4–6).

"I delight to do your will, O my God; your law is within my heart" (Psalm 40:8).

Consider journaling about these questions, or use them to spark discussion with a group of friends:

- Think about what you most crave—solitude, perhaps; freedom from pain; freedom from anxiety; a better relationship with your children—and what keeps you from it. Could it be that the Lord desires you to pursue the very thing you are seeing as an impediment to what you want?

- People called Genoveva "the angel of solitude." What moniker would you like to be known or remembered by and why?

Praying with Genoveva

St. Genoveva, help me to find the courage to serve as the Father deserves. Ask him to provide the grace I need to do his will.

Resources

- Visit the site for Genoveva's congregation to learn about how the saint's work goes on today.
- View a brief video from the Diocese of Segorbe-Castellon, Spain, from the celebration of Genoveva's feast day in 2019.
- Learn more about St. Joaquina Vedruna de Mas, whose Carmelites of Charity sisters cared for Genoveva during her teen years.

CHAPTER 17

Léonie Aviat
Being a Peacemaker

The Basics

Born September 16, 1844, in France | Died January 10, 1914, in Italy

Canonized November 25, 2001 | Feast Day: January 10

Léonie's Radical Gift

St. Léonie Aviat loved serving the poor as an Oblate Sister of St. Francis de Sales, and she was the community's first superior general. Just a few years later, a successor would send her away to a different assignment; that woman's successor, who also had been one of the original members of the community, demoted her. Four years later, Léonie became superior general, a position she held until her death. She accepted all these twists and turns with humility—and radical confidence that God, not she or the other women, was in control.

Léonie's World

France experienced internal and external strife during much of Léonie's life, including the beginning of the 1848 revolutions that rolled across Europe. She had just turned fourteen when the Blessed Mother appeared to Bernadette Soubirous at Lourdes. (Bernadette was nine months older than Léonie.)

Léonie's Radical Path to Holiness

Léonie spent her early years in Sézanne, a pleasant community about seventy miles east of Paris. When she was eleven, her parents sent her to the Visitation convent boarding school, about forty miles away in

Troyes. There, she encountered Fr. Louis Brisson, the school's chaplain with whom she would be linked in ministry for decades to come.

Fr. Brisson was mightily concerned about the lives, not to mention the souls, of girls who were leaving rural France to take positions in Troyes' textile mills. In 1858 or 1859, he opened a center where young women would be safe from the city's worldly temptations, even if just for a few hours. In Léonie, he saw someone with a strong faith who potentially could speak to the girls in ways he could not, since she was near their age.

Her school years finished, Léonie went home to Sézanne. She found herself at loose ends; her desire was to become a woman religious, but the superior at her convent school, Mother Marie de Sales Chappuis, had told her to wait. Her family had arranged for Léonie to be married, but when her father's business failed, her would-be husband was no longer interested in having her as his wife. And so, she waited.

The story is that one day Léonie went to pick up her mother's glasses from a shop and felt called to help young people like the ones she saw working there. Whether or not that actually happened, we do know that in the meantime, Mother Chappuis, a Salesian spirituality devotee, had been gently (or not so gently) nudging Fr. Brisson to formally found a community to support Troyes's at-risk workers. In 1866, Léonie and a former classmate, Lucie Canuet, became the managers of one of the centers Father Brisson had opened; on October 30, 1868, they began their novitiates in the new Oblates Sisters of St. Francis de Sales community as Srs. Françoise de Sales and Jeanne-Marie. Four years later, Sr. Françoise became superior general.

Whether it was assisting Franco-Prussian War refugees or factory workers, or coping with the merger with another community, the sisters were kept busy. (As a point of reference, Troyes's population in 1872 was nearly thirty-five thousand; by 1886, it was nearly fifty thousand, an increase of about 43 percent.)

Internal strife clouded the women's ministry beginning in 1879 when Françoise's term was complete. The new superior, from the merged community, lasted only two years; her successor thought it best to send Sr. Françoise to rescue the oblates' activities at a Paris boarding school a hundred miles away. Her first foray into formal education was not initially welcomed, but ultimately the community and students there accepted her.

Meanwhile, back in Troyes, tensions escalated, with the local bishop opposing Fr. Brisson's efforts to expand the Salesian male and female communities beyond the diocese. And, in 1884, Jeanne-Marie, whom Françoise had struggled to love, became superior general. Five years later, Jeanne-Marie recalled Françoise to Troyes, which was seen as a demotion. Françoise accepted the reassignment with grace and poise, and in September 1893, again found herself as superior general, a position she would hold until her death.

At Léonie's canonization, St. John Paul II said she "put prayer and union with God, where she found the light and the energy to overcome trials and difficulties, and to persevere to the end of her life in the life of faith, desiring to be led by the Lord."[31]

Léonie's Wisdom

"Oh my God, let my happiness be found in sacrificing my desires for you!"[32]

Living Radically Today

After she got her bachelor's degree, Angie was all set to teach. Except, in short order, she learned that was not her gift, got married, had a child, got divorced, and moved far away from family and friends to get an advanced degree. While she hasn't had a perfect life since, it's been full of love: a second, Spirit-led husband; three more children and a half-dozen grandchildren; more friends than she can count.

One of Angie's very first jobs upon earning her advanced degree was with a brand-new government agency. Forty years later, after a career of increasing responsibilities, she's returned to lead the agency where she started, and not everyone is happy about it.

While the agency's mission hasn't changed in the intervening years, the way some of the employees regard it has. There's a sense that the agency exists for them rather than for the taxpayers. When Angie shares her plans and strategies for the coming years, the employees don't always agree with her and are quite vocal about it, inside the agency and publicly.

Just as Léonie was gracious when her vocation took her in and out of leadership roles, sometimes at the whim of people she found challenging, Angie is gracious to her employees and those outside the agency who criticize her. She has town-hall meetings and addresses employees' comments and concerns there or in internal blog posts. She spends time one-on-one with even the most challenging among her staff and hears their complaints, some of which are far beyond her (or anyone on earth's) power to address in the way they'd like. She incorporates their ideas where she can, explains why that can't always happen, and communicates the bigger picture.

The key, I think, is that she doesn't let the harsh words and judgment thrown at her encroach on all the joy in her personal life too much. She has hosted an open-to-all weekly prayer group for years, and she has been a daily communicant since she took this professional leadership role. She and her husband remain active in the Catholic organization through which they met decades ago. Angie is confident that, as she often says to friends who are worried or anxious about something, "God's got this covered!"

RADICAL THOUGHTS

Here are a couple of verses to contemplate as you think about Léonie's life:

"But the meek shall inherit the land, and delight themselves in abundant prosperity" (Psalm 37:11).

"My child, do not let these escape from your sight: keep sound wisdom and prudence, and they will be life for your soul and adornment for your neck" (Proverbs 3:21–22).

Consider journaling about these questions, or use them to spark discussion with a group of friends:

- We all have at least one person who gets under our skin because he makes judgmental statements about us, because she all but flat-out says she's a better mother, because he connived and lied to get that promotion that should have been ours. How does God view such a person? What does he find to love in this person?

- Consider tracking all the negative things you say (or hear) about yourself in a single day. Burn the page at the end of the day and resolve not to say (or take to heart) the same things tomorrow.

PRAYING WITH LÉONIE

St. Léonie, help me to accept and love people as Christ accepts and loves them. May I not let them serve as impediments to doing what the Lord asks of me.

RESOURCES

- The Oblate Sisters of St. Francis de Sales site offers biographies on Léonie and Father Brisson along with information on the sisters' work today.

- The October 2005 edition of The Abbey of Saint-Joseph de Clairval newsletter featured a detailed profile of the saint.
- Louis Brisson was beatified in September 2012; a related site provides much detail on the work he did with Léonie.

CHAPTER 18

KATHARINE DREXEL
Getting Out of Our Comfort Zone

THE BASICS

Born November 26, 1858, in the United States | Died March 3, 1955, in the United States

Canonized October 1, 2000 | Feast Day: March 3

KATHARINE'S RADICAL GIFT

St. Katharine Drexel was raised in a loving family that had plenty of money and philanthropic spirit. But when Katharine's request for missionaries was answered by the suggestion that she become one herself, she discerned and gave a radical yes.

KATHARINE'S WORLD

The changes in the United States during Katharine's long life are breathtaking; consider that James Buchanan was president when she was born, and Dwight Eisenhower was in the White House when she died. The country went from thirty-two states to forty-eight; its population, from 31.4 million (including four million enslaved) to nearly 166 million. Transportation went from passenger train and horse and carriage to automobile and commercial air travel. Katharine's life also spanned six papacies, from Pius IX to Pius XII.

KATHARINE'S RADICAL PATH TO HOLINESS

It seemed like a perfectly reasonable, Spirit-filled request. Katharine came from a line of socially conscious philanthropists, one of the country's wealthiest families. A trip with her two sisters to the western United States had illumined the need for missionaries to serve among Native American communities. Where better to take her request than to Pope Leo XIII?

"Yes" was the only answer Katharine expected at that January 1887 private audience in Rome.

But instead, Leo XIII asked why she didn't become a missionary herself. (Leo XIII was a pope of memorable answers; later in 1887, he would tell fifteen-year-old Thérèse of Lisieux to listen to the superiors when she begged him to get her into Carmel; almost exactly two years after the audience with Katharine, he would tell Frances Cabrini to take her ministry to the United States, not China.)

Katharine left in tears, very confused.

The concept of being a missionary herself was not something that appealed to Katharine. Oh, she'd considered becoming a contemplative nun back in her teens, but everyone, including her spiritual director, advised against it. In abandoning the thought, she wrote in a moment of honest self-reflection that she didn't know if she could live with the deprivations, including the lack of privacy, that religious life entailed.

And after all, she'd had a lifelong example of the difference laypeople could make in the world. Her banker father had served on numerous charity boards in Philadelphia before his death less than a year earlier, and a share of his multimillion-dollar estate had gone to charitable causes. Her beloved stepmother, who had died a painful death from cancer in 1883, had opened the family's mansion on a regular basis to those in need, providing fuel, food, and clothing (and tutoring and Sunday school classes taught by the three Drexel girls). The daughters had followed those examples as adults.

But become a missionary herself?

That fall Katharine and her sisters went to some Native American missions in what is now South Dakota, including one where

Katharine was already funding a school. There they visited with her spiritual director and former pastor, Bishop James O'Connor, the region's first bishop; Monsignor Joseph Stephan, Bureau of Catholic Indian Missions director; Chief Red Cloud, a Lakota Catholic; and other Lakota. The following year, they visited three reservations in the Northwest. The trips showed Katharine anew the peoples' physical and spiritual needs.

The day she turned thirty—November 26, 1888—Katharine wrote her spiritual director to say she had made up her mind. Against his earlier advice, she would become a woman religious. Letters flew between them, with Bishop O'Connor urging her to form a community of missionary sisters. Finally, after a March 1889 retreat, she said yes.

In May 1889, Katharine became a postulant at a Sisters of Mercy convent in Pittsburgh. Two years later, she took her first vows. A year after that, she opened the first Sisters of the Blessed Sacrament convent in suburban Philadelphia, with a boarding school for African American children on the property. There was a bomb threat, but Katharine soldiered on. In the next thirty-seven years, she and the other Blessed Sacrament sisters continued to persevere despite arson, threats from the Ku Klux Klan, and more. They established missions and schools for Native American and African American children as well as Xavier University in New Orleans, the United States' only historically black Catholic college.

In 1935, Katharine suffered a severe stroke, which precipitated her withdrawal from active ministry. She spent her final twenty years at the motherhouse. It's estimated that her personal contributions to her community's ministries totaled more than $500 million in today's dollars.

KATHARINE'S WISDOM

"If we wish to serve God and love our neighbor well, we must manifest our joy in the service we render to Him and them. Let us open wide our hearts. It is joy which invites us. Press forward and fear nothing."[33]

LIVING RADICALLY TODAY

Joan literally was making out like a bandit. Oh, she was by no means as rich as Katharine Drexel, but she'd had a very successful two decades as what's called a "Beltway bandit," working for a large company that provides consulting services to the U.S. government. She worked in contracts and finance, skills that are always in demand. She had a nice house. She loved traveling. She was involved in a wide variety of ministries at her parish and beyond.

But something was telling her that wasn't all God wanted from her. Joan prayed. She talked with trusted advisers. She came to believe that she was being called to parish work—not as a volunteer, but as an employee, a shift that would mean a substantial change in both her income and living standard.

She decided her only answer could be yes. So Joan began scaling back on the little niceties in her life. She sold her house. She moved in with her sister's family. About ten years ago, she became a parish adult faith formation director. More recently, she put that background in contracts and finance to work to earn a master's degree in church management.

If you added up the hours Joan spends in parish activities—do adult faith formation directors ever get a weekend off?—her own ministries, and work she does as a wellness coach, I suspect she's working more hours than she ever did as a government consultant.

Her life is not devoid of fun; she still follows her beloved Atlanta Falcons football team, goes to outdoor concerts and shows several times each summer, and travels with her family. But she has a sense of calm that comes only when we live the life God desires for us. She and Katharine Drexel teach us that saying yes to God can be difficult at first, but always leads us to joy and peace.

RADICAL THOUGHTS

Here are a couple of verses to contemplate as you think about Katharine's life:

"He must increase, but I must decrease" (John 3:30).

"Let your steadfast love become my comfort according to your promise to your servant" (Psalm 119:76).

Consider journaling about these questions, or use them to spark discussion with a group of friends:

- What question is the Lord asking you that you'd prefer not to answer? What would it take for you to do so?

- Katharine didn't think she could give up some of the trappings of wealth, including privacy. Once she said yes to becoming a sister, she found it easier to say yes to other sacrifices, such as giving up sugar. Consider making a sacrifice, even if it's just for a few days, of a small personal indulgence. Do you feel different after doing this?

PRAYING WITH KATHARINE

St. Katharine, you spent time discerning God's will. I ask for your help in finding the faith and courage to do the same.

RESOURCES

- A Philadelphia TV station has put together an excellent video that focuses on the saint's early years.

- Visit the Sisters of the Blessed Sacrament site to learn more about Katharine and the good work the sisters do today.
- Take a virtual visit to the St. Katharine Drexel Shrine at the Cathedral Basilica in Philadelphia.

CHAPTER 19

JOSEPHINE BAKHITA
Forgiving as Christ Does

THE BASICS

Born about 1869 in Sudan | Died February 8, 1947, in Italy

Canonized October 1, 2000 | Feast Day: February 8

JOSEPHINE'S RADICAL GIFT

Slave traders took away her name and her family. She was kidnapped, beaten, and scarred. And yet, when asked what she would say to her persecutors if she met them again, Josephine said she would thank them, because without them she would not have discovered her faith and her vocation.

JOSEPHINE'S WORLD

Raids to enslave Sudanese during Josephine's childhood were not uncommon, and they continued after the practice was outlawed in 1924. In a 2018 report, the U.S. Department of State noted that while Sudan today is working to eliminate human trafficking, the country's efforts still do not fully meet minimum standards.

JOSEPHINE'S RADICAL PATH TO HOLINESS

Even in the worst of times, the times she was struck every day, the time her enslavers made her walk for miles on end, the times she was turned over to yet another enslaver, Josephine had always wondered: *The sun. The moon. The stars. Who had put them all there? Who was in charge of them? It must be someone very great indeed.*

But then, the girl didn't have a whole of time to think about theology or philosophy. Mainly she focused on survival. The men who had taken her away from her family when she was seven or eight had scared her so badly that she forgot her name and birthdate. They had a cruel sense of humor; they dubbed her *Bakhita*, "fortunate one" in Arabic.

The first enslavers made her walk barefoot for a day, then hid her away for more than a month in a dark hut before "selling" her to someone else. During the next seven years or so, at least four more people would use and abuse her. One, she said, hurt her every single, solitary day. At a Turkish general's home, someone used flour to draw more than one hundred patterns on her body, then cut them into her skin, then rubbed them with salt to ensure permanent scarring. Bakhita couldn't move for three months after this savagery.

She still wondered from time to time about that larger world beyond her suffering, the one with the majesty of the sun, the moon, and the stars. It must have seemed far beyond her reach.

In 1883, the Italian vice consul in Khartoum encountered Bakhita at the home where she had been so gruesomely scarred, and he acquired her. Bakhita remembered him as the first enslaver who didn't hurt her. When political issues required the family to return to Italy, they took Bakhita along. She was then "gifted" to Augusto Michieli, a Venetian businessman and friend of the vice counsel.

One of Bakhita's main jobs for the Michielis was to serve as nanny for their little girl, called Mimmina. When Mimmina was around two years old, her parents decided to move to Sudan permanently, and they sold their estate in Italy. But some details remained to be settled, and the Michielis didn't want to subject the child to any more travel than was necessary. Finally, at the recommendation of the couple's business administrator, it was decided that Bakhita and Mimmina would live at the Canossian Sisters' boarding school in

Venice. The administrator also provided Bakhita with two gifts: a small silver crucifix, and the story of the crucifixion and Resurrection.

At the boarding school parlor, Bakhita saw a larger crucifix, one on which Jesus's wounds were visible, just like her own scars. She began taking religious instruction with the Canossians. When Mrs. Michieli returned nine months later, Bakhita refused to return to Sudan with her. A legal battle ensued, and in November 1889, an Italian court found that Bakhita was free, as laws in Italy did not recognize slavery. Two months later, Bakhita received a different type of freedom: she was initiated into the Church and took the name Josephine Margaret Fortunata.

As Josephine's faith deepened, she found herself called to religious life. She became a Canossian novitiate at the end of 1893 and made her first vows in 1896. Josephine was assigned to a convent about sixty miles away in Schio, which was her residence for most of the rest of her life. There was no duty she would not take on: cook, sacristan, doorkeeper, weaver. Josephine's writing and reading skills remained limited, and another sister was assigned to take down her stories. Interest in her journey resulted in new roles of speaking (with another sister providing most of the talking) on behalf of missions to Africa and helping sisters prepare for work there.

Josephine was confined to a wheelchair in her final years, and she died of pulmonary congestion. She never remembered her original name. After the day she was abducted, she never again saw her parents or any of her six siblings. And yet, when she was asked what she would do if she encountered those who had tortured her and taken everything but her human dignity, she was quick to answer that she would kneel and kiss their hands. If it had not been for them, she said, she would not have been a Christian or a Canossian.

JOSEPHINE'S WISDOM

"In God's will, there is great peace."[34]

LIVING RADICALLY TODAY

I'd just paid off more than a hundred thousand dollars in marital debt over the course of three years, and I had saved up enough money to pay cash for a two-week trip with my sister to Romania and Istanbul.

There was just one problem: I was seeing flashing lights in my right eye. I went to my ophthalmologist, who ran all kinds of tests and said to watch it. I asked if it was safe to take my trip. He told me about his father-in-law, a Romanian émigré, and said to drink a Dracula beer for him.

The train was pulling into Istanbul when everything went black in my right eye. I called the ophthalmologist, who said it sounded like a detached retina and told me to see a specialist. But due to Muslim and Jewish holy days, specialists weren't even answering their phones. I decided we might as well stay the remaining five days. I called my prayer group—what else could I do in this situation?

I saw the ophthalmologist the morning after I returned. He hadn't even bothered to pull my chart to see which eye was involved. But he did connect me with a first-rate retinal specialist, who was working on a Saturday. This specialist advised waiting until Monday for surgery (a better team would be working, and so much time had already passed) and said while my vision would improve, he couldn't promise how much.

It was more than a week before the ophthalmologist called to see how I was doing. I didn't yell at him; I just hung up. He then contacted the specialist and accused him of attempting to drive a wedge between us; I wrote the ophthalmologist a detailed letter explaining how he had done that all by himself.

Time passed. A second surgery returned my eye to 20/20 vision, which it hadn't been since I was seven years old. The retina specialist gave the credit to my prayer group.

The following spring at a routine exam, I commented that, in some ways, the detachment had been a blessing.

"This is Lent for you, right, when Catholics seek and give forgiveness?" the specialist asked.

Sensing what was coming next, I said yes.

"Maybe it's time to write another letter."

So I did. In it, I told the ophthalmologist about my progress and said that I forgave him. I never heard back from him. I'm OK with that. On a much smaller scale than Bakhita, the experience helped me to learn that joy can come from seemingly hopeless situations, and forgiving those who were indifferent or fostered our suffering is a gift that blesses everyone involved.

RADICAL THOUGHTS

Here are a couple of verses to contemplate as you think about Josephine's life:

"Whenever you stand praying, forgive, if you have anything against anyone; so that your Father in heaven may also forgive you your trespasses" (Mark 11:25).

"Blessed are the merciful, for they will receive mercy" (Matthew 5:7).

Consider journaling about these questions, or use them to spark discussion with a group of friends:

- Write a message of forgiveness to someone who injured you, physically, spiritually, or emotionally. Send it if it's safe to do so.

- Forgiving ourselves can be even harder than forgiving others. Consider talking with a spiritual director or other counselor about something you have done that you continue to dwell on. Do you believe your sin is so great that God cannot forgive it?

Praying with Josephine

St. Josephine, your radical forgiveness awes me. Help me to extend the same mercy to those who have harmed me.

Resources

- View Sister Miriam James Heidland's video about the saint.
- Visit the site for Josephine's community, the Canossian Institute of Schio, to learn more about the sisters' works and about how Josephine continues to touch lives today.
- Read Benedict XVI's 2007 encyclical letter *Spe Salvi* (Saved in Hope), which includes references to Josephine's story.

CHAPTER 20

María Natividad Venegas de la Torre
Extending Hospitality to All

The Basics

Born September 8, 1868, in Mexico | Died July 30, 1959, in Mexico
Canonized May 21, 2000 | Feast Day: July 30

María's Radical Gift

Mexico's first female saint went from nurse to pharmacist to accountant to director of the Guadalajara hospital where her community did its first ministry. María's confidence in the Lord and her hospitality kept the hospital open and assisting all amid religious persecution.

María's World

The Church's relationship with the Mexican government ebbed and flowed during María's lifetime, even as Catholicism remained the country's primary religion. Church leadership had opposed the 1910–1920 civil war, in which revolutionaries prevailed. When anticlerical laws were instituted in 1926, what is known as the Cristero Rebellion broke out. It lasted three years and resulted in about ninety thousand deaths. The laws remained on the books for years afterward but were seldom enforced.

María's Radical Path to Holiness

Choices—María had choices, almost an embarrassing number of choices for a woman of her time. The youngest of twelve children, she received a rich education in religion and literature at home. She enjoyed writing and would pen some materials about the west central Mexican area in which she grew up. María also had a gift for working with children, and she served as an informal teacher. But it wasn't enough. So, when she was thirty, María joined a lay association, the Daughters of Mary, dedicated to doing good works. Members consecrated themselves to purity under the Blessed Virgin's guidance.

Meanwhile, the Hospital of the Sacred Heart had opened in 1886 in what was previously a Guadalupe home, with just ten beds. The local diocese bought a plot behind the house to expand the facility and ground was broken in late 1889. In May 1893, the first Mass was celebrated in the hospital chapel by the local bishop, whose brother, also a priest, was the hospital director.

It wasn't long before María's and the hospital's futures became forever linked. The Daughters of Mary were offering an Ignatian retreat during Advent in 1905, and María's spiritual director strongly encouraged her to take part. He believed she was being called to live as a cloistered woman religious.

Instead, shortly after the retreat, María joined a nascent community of women at the hospital. That community eventually became the Daughters of the Sacred Heart of Jesus of Guadalajara. Initially, she was a nurse, then a pharmacist, and then the hospital's accountant. She became the community's vicar in 1912, then served as superior general and hospital supervisor from 1921 until 1954. In religious life, she was known as María de Jesús Sacramentado, or Madre Nati.

Of those thirty-plus years in leadership, most would regard 1926–1929 as her most challenging. Tensions between the Catholic Church and the Mexican government boiled over when President Plutarco Elías Calles signed a law to enforce anti-Catholic provisions of the country's constitution. Monasteries, convents, and schools were shuttered; Church property was seized; priests seen in clerical clothing in public were subject to stiff fines. An uprising known as the Cristero Rebellion ensued, resulting in about ninety thousand deaths in three years.

The rebellion came to the hospital. But instead of engaging with the government soldiers in a way that would heighten the tension (and risk the hospital's doors being closed), Madre Nati met them with courtesy and hospitality. No one who needed attention was turned away, Catholic or non-Catholic, military or civilian. She and her sisters managed to save the Eucharist from desecration by carefully hiding it in their beehives. As a result of her efforts, the hospital remained open throughout the conflict.

Though she felt ill-equipped for the task, Madre Nati had completed her community's constitutions, or governing documents, a couple of years before the Cristero conflict began. A year after it was over, the community was formally approved.

In 1954, her time as superior general completed and sixteen houses founded, Madre Nati continued to see patients and to live with her community. A stroke in 1955 cost her the ability to speak for a time, but she eventually regained it. Fittingly, she died at the Hospital of the Sacred Heart. Her remains are housed there, as are some of the items she kept in her cell.

MARÍA'S WISDOM
"Charity enters heaven when humility opens the door."[35]

LIVING RADICALLY TODAY
You would think that raising five children in a cozy suburban home would be plenty for any mother. But then, you wouldn't know Janice.

She laughs now about how she had five or six—or maybe it was seven?—of her children's friends living with her family at one point or another. She and her husband took them in because they had no place else to go. And besides, if you're already feeding a family of seven, another plate or two—or maybe it was three?—really isn't a big deal. Or at least Janice didn't think so.

Janice's kids—including the temporary ones—are all grown now, and many of them have kids of their own. Her charity and hospitality continue in other ways. Her home is always open for gatherings; it's not magazine-picture perfect, but the warmth is evident from the moment you sink into one of the comfy couches. She doesn't like to talk much about it, but her fundraising efforts were critical in keeping a pro-life medical practice in business. She helped to reform a couple of Catholic organizations (she's on the boards for both now, of course) and brought them back to health, in no small part by inviting people to activities, and greeting them with a hearty welcome, just as Jesus would do. Some people might think Janice just can't say no, but that's not the case at all. She selects her ministries carefully, but once she selects one, she's all in.

I've asked Janice more than once how she manages to do all this, plus nurture her marriage, plus work a demanding job that has an hour-a-day commute. She usually laughs and says something about being a mother—or about God's grace. As I've watched her over the years, I think it also has something to do with balancing her service with her prayer life. She goes on a silent retreat at least once a year. She puts time with God ahead of any social media activity. (And you're more likely to get a quick phone call from her than a tweet, text, or email.)

Janice's place isn't in a physical hospital like María's was. But make no mistake: in a world where people can be quick to judge, condemn, and dismiss each other based on the way they vote, the way they dress,

even the way they take the Eucharist, Janice is there to welcome—
and to guide the way to divine healing through community.

Radical Thoughts

Here are a couple of verses to contemplate as you think about María's
life:

> "Whoever welcomes you welcomes me, and whoever
> welcomes me welcomes the one who sent me" (Matthew
> 10:40).
>
> "Contribute to the needs of the saints; extend hospitality to
> strangers" (Romans 12:13).

Consider journaling about these questions, or use them to spark
discussion with a group of friends:

- The only "side" we ever have to take in a conflict is the Lord's.
  Think about ways you can reflect him—and Madre Nati's
  hospitality—in defusing disagreements between your children,
  coworkers, or friends.

- What place is most identified with your good works? Your
  home is a fine answer! If a plaque were to be placed there, what
  would it read?

Praying with María

Saint María, help me to fling my arms open to welcome those who
don't know Jesus or who have turned away from him and don't know
how to find him. Help me to show them Jesus in a way that will
touch their souls.

Resources

- View a video on the saint's life, including photos, created by
  Azteca América, a Spanish-language network that covers the
  United States and northern Mexico.

- Read the reminisces of one of the saint's great-nephews in an article in the Knights of Columbus's *Columbia* publication.
- Visit the website for her community, Daughters of the Sacred Heart of Jesus, to learn about the good work they do today.

CHAPTER 21

MARIA FAUSTINA KOWALSKA
Laser-Focused on the Lord

THE BASICS

Born August 25, 1905, in Poland | Died October 5, 1938, in Poland
Canonized April 30, 2000 | Feast Day: October 5

FAUSTINA'S RADICAL GIFT

It's human nature to desire to be well-liked and understood. Many of those around Faustina, including some of the women in her own community, saw her single-minded drive to bring the Lord's Divine Mercy message to the world as egotistical and delusional. Faustina didn't care what anyone other than Jesus thought of her, and she radically embraced being his messenger.

FAUSTINA'S WORLD

You wouldn't have found Poland on a map when Faustina was born; the place where her parents lived was then part of Russia. Poland came back into existence when she was thirteen. In the week before her death, Nazi troops marched into Czechoslovakia's Sudetenland under an agreement with the British, French, and Italian governments.

FAUSTINA'S RADICAL PATH

The Lord had a special mission for Faustina. She'd been aware of it for some time, and he had shown her through visions the priest who would help her fulfill that mission. Now, weeks before her twenty-eighth birthday, Father Michael Sopoćko was in front of her, but he didn't seem to be taking her seriously—just like so many people before him. That, however, did not change her certainty that he was the one sent to help her.

Helena Kowalska's large family didn't have much; in fact, she sometimes wasn't able to go to Mass because there weren't enough appropriate dresses. Educational opportunities were limited. But like her father, she had a deep prayer life and a strong sense of religious obligation.

Helena was fifteen and had already started working as a domestic when she told her parents she was being called to enter a convent. They said no, in part due to the fact there was no money for a dowry. While she was obedient then, everything changed just a few years later. Helena was at a dance with her sister when she had a vision of Jesus asking her why she kept putting him off. Shaken, she went to a nearby cathedral, where Jesus appeared again and told her to go to Warsaw, eighty-five miles away, and join a convent. Helena said good-bye to her sister, let an uncle know she was leaving, and got on a train with only the clothes she was wearing.

However, the women religious of Warsaw seemed not to have received the same message from the Lord. The young woman met with rejection after rejection. Finally, the Sisters of Our Lady of Mercy agreed to consider her if she could cover the cost of her habit. Helena worked for months until that was accomplished and then entered the convent. It took just weeks for her to question whether it was the right place for her—there was not enough prayer time, for one thing. But Jesus told her to stay, and so she did. She received her habit and the name Sister Faustina on April 30, 1926.

Over the next five years, Faustina was moved from convent to convent. Some of the other sisters found her judgmental; others thought she considered herself superior to them; still others believed her lazy. (She likely was in the early stages of tuberculosis by 1930, and the resulting coughing and chest pains kept her from working.)

She seemed indifferent to their opinions.

Faustina was in her cell on the evening of February 22, 1931, when Jesus appeared, dressed in white with two rays shining from him. He provided some specific instructions: Faustina was to have an image of him painted with the words *Jesus, I trust in you*. The image should be venerated in the convent chapel, and eventually throughout the world. The first Sunday after Easter would be proclaimed the feast of mercy.

The sharing of this vision opened Faustina up to further criticism within the community, and there were some questions about whether she should be allowed to remain, but ultimately she took her final vows.

Faustina arrived in Vilnius, Lithuania, in late May 1933, and soon thereafter met Father Michael Sopoćko, who had recently added the role as convent confessor to his teaching duties at a nearby university. The first time she went to confession with him, she shared her conversations with Jesus. After initially doubting her—to the point that he ordered her to have a psychiatric workup—Father Sopoćko did indeed prove to be the priest the Lord had sent. It was at his direction that she wrote what would become *The Diary of St. Maria Faustina Kowalska: Divine Mercy in My Soul*. Through him, the original Divine Mercy artist was engaged. Father Sopoćko delivered the first homily on Divine Mercy on the Sunday after Easter in 1935, with Faustina in attendance.

Three-and-a-half years later, Faustina was dead. She did not live to see the Divine Mercy spread worldwide through the efforts of Father Sopoćko and others; then banned; then revived through the promotion of Kraków Archbishop Karol Wojtyła. In 2000, as John Paul II, he canonized Faustina and designated the Sunday after Easter as Divine Mercy Sunday. But none of it might have happened if Faustina had not radically embraced her role as the Lord's messenger, regardless of the personal slings and arrows that came along with it.

Faustina's Wisdom

"My sanctity and perfection consist in the close union of my will with the will of God. God never violates our free will."[36]

Living Radically Today

I thought about it every day during Lent that year. I was writing a book on women saints and the Beatitudes, and that was when I first learned about how Jesus told Faustina to leave the dance and get on that train and go to Warsaw, and so she did, without sleeping on it or talking to her parents or anything else. I admired her surrender and her instant yes. I must have processed it dozens of times with one of my dearest friends.

"Duffy," I said, "what if I've missed the train? What happens? Is there another train later? Or do I go to hell?"

"Mel, don't worry," she said over and over. "You're already on the train. You write for God. You speak for God. You do service for God. You're on the train."

But I knew I wasn't, not completely. For a dozen years, I'd had an off-and-on relationship with a man who lived about seventy-five miles away, and we were in an on-again time. We both knew it wasn't a relationship that would lead to marriage. I worried about whether that would make me miss the train, but not enough to do anything about it. I kept telling myself that God would find a way to make it clear that the relationship displeased him if it really did…and I hoped and prayed that he wouldn't.

The weekend before Pentecost, I was at a Walk to Emmaus retreat in the North Carolina mountains. I went thinking I would be a speaker, but when I arrived, the organizers had a surprise for me: since I hadn't done my own Walk, I'd also be a participant. I'm not much for surprises, but I said sure and did all the things one does on a Walk that are supposed to help you grow in love and trust of God.

I was fascinated by one of the other participants. She was slight and could have been anywhere from forty to eighty years old. She spoke little, but she seemed to listen carefully to all the presentations and conversations. During a reconciliation service Saturday night, she rolled herself up into a little ball on the floor and sobbed. When I walked over to see if she needed help, the woman extended her arm to ward me off.

I had traveled to North Carolina with a friend, and we both needed to leave at midday Sunday. As we were attempting to slip away, the woman I had seen the night before approached me and asked if we could speak privately. When we stepped outside, she said quietly but with confidence, "I have a message for you from God. He desires you to move to a higher slope."

I was silent most of the four hundred miles back to Virginia. I'd prayed for a sign. Well, God had accommodated me.

The romance ended once and for all without drama or tears or angry words—without words at all, actually. Maybe God had spoken to him as well.

I emailed that woman in North Carolina a week later to thank her. This is what she wrote back, in part:

> "Higher slopes"…they are more difficult. I know little, but I can affirm only this, the desire grows and the difficulty contains a sort of delicious pain. I rarely share these descriptive words, but your face reflects this desire. I will pray."

I am grateful that she, like Faustina, was willing to be God's messenger, unconcerned about what the recipient's response might be. These days, not only do I listen for God's messengers, I pray for the bravery and wisdom to serve as a messenger as well.

Radical Thoughts

Here are a couple of verses to contemplate as you think about Faustina's life:

"I can do all things through him who strengthens me" (Philippians 4:13).

"Finally, be strong in the Lord and in the strength of his power" (Ephesians 6:10).

Consider journaling about these questions, or use them to spark discussion with a group of friends:

- Are you reluctant to say yes to a request from the Lord because it might cost you prestige, popularity, or friendships? Are those things worth the risk of losing him?

- Does a friend or acquaintance sometimes seem a little "out there," talking about conversations with God, the Blessed Virgin, or some other heavenly being? Do you discount his or her accounts?

Praying with Faustina

St. Faustina, help me to emulate your laser-beam focus on Jesus and to set aside the things in my life that threaten to blur my vision.

Resources

- See a Knights of Columbus video including Faustina's canonization and some images from her life and photos of her family's farm home and other plans where she lived.
- Visit the site for the Congregation of the Sisters of Our Lady of Mercy.

- Learn more about devotion to Divine Mercy today at Krakow's Basilica of Divine Mercy.
- Learn about how the message Faustina received is shared through the National Shrine of the Divine Mercy in Stockbridge, Massachusetts.

More Radical Women

Want to know about other twentieth-century women canonized in this century and what they can teach us? This list is current as of January 2020.

Nazaria Ignacia March Mesa (born January 10, 1889, in Spain; died July 6, 1943, in Argentina; canonized October 14, 2018; feast day: July 6). As a child, her devotion to the Lord and desire to become a woman religious were so strong that her parents grew weary of hearing about both. Founder of the Missionary Crusaders of the Church.

María de la Purísima Salvat Romero (born February 20, 1926, in Spain; died October 31, 1998, in Spain; canonized October 18, 2015; feast day: September 18). The convent rules were important to her, and she made sure everyone including herself, followed them to a T. Member of the Sisters of the Company of the Cross.

Marie-Alphonsine Danil Ghattas (born October 4, 1843, in Palestine; died March 25, 1927, in Palestine; canonized May 17, 2015; feast day: March 25). She had such a special relationship of the Blessed Virgin that she established a congregation devoted to the Rosary, the first Palestinian community of women religious. Founder of the Holy Order of the Rosary.

Maria Cristina of the Immaculate Conception Brando (born May 1, 1856, in Italy; died January 20, 1906, in Italy; canonized May 17, 2015; feast day: January 20). She was devoted to the Lord's sacrifice for us and to the gift of the Eucharist, spending hours in Adoration. Founder of the Sisters, Expiatory Victims of Jesus in the Blessed Sacrament.

María Guadalupe Garcia Zavala (born April 27, 1878, in Mexico; died June 24, 1963, in Mexico; canonized May 12, 2013; feast day: June 24). She was in love and engaged to be married. Then she realized she loved Jesus even more, and he had another plan for her. Founder of Handmaids of St. Mary Margaret and the Poor, see a Spanish-language video with images from all stages of her life.

María del Monte Carmelo Sallés y Barangueras (born April 9, 1848, in Spain; died July 25, 1911, in Spain; canonized October 21, 2012; feast day: December 6). Her focus was on human dignity and equality, in particular for women. Founder of the Missionary Sisters of the Immaculate Conception of Mary.

Bonifacia Rodríguez y Castro (born June 6, 1837, in Spain; died August 8, 1905, in Spain; canonized October 23, 2011; feast day: August 8). From her childhood days observing her tailor father, she understood the value of work. Cofounder of the Servants of St. Joseph.

Giulia Salzano (born October 13, 1846, in Italy; died May 17, 1929, in Italy; canonized October 17, 2010; feast day: May 17). She loved teaching people—children and adults alike—about the beauties of our faith. Founder of the Catechetical Sisters of the Sacred Heart of Jesus.

Cándida María of Jesús (born May 31, 1845, in Spain; died August 9, 1912, in Spain; canonized October 17, 2010; feast day: August 9). Growing up, she had little money and little education. As a woman religious, she helped the poor and established schools across her country. Founder of the Daughters of Jesus.

Geltrude Comensoli (born January 18, 1847, in Italy; died February 18, 1903, in Italy; canonized April 26, 2009; feast day: February 18). Her focus was on adoration of the Eucharist. She was convinced to expand her community's ministry to help young working women. Founder of the Sacramentine Sisters of Bergamo.

María Bernarda Bütler (born May 28, 1848, in Switzerland; died May 19, 1924, in Colombia; canonized October 12, 2008; feast day: May 19). Just after her fortieth birthday, she and six other sisters left Switzerland for Ecuador. Ministry in South America wasn't always easy, but she did it for decades. Founder of the Franciscan Missionaries of Mary Help of Christians.

Ursula Ledóchowska (born April 17, 1865, in Austria; died May 29, 1939, n Italy; canonized May 18, 2003; feast day: May 29). For a time, she and her sister nuns were "undercover" in Russia, because they weren't allowed to wear their habits. Founder of the Ursulines of the Agonizing Heart of Jesus.

Angela of the Cross Guerrero y González (born January 30, 1846, in Spain; died March 2, 1932, in Spain; canonized May 4, 2003; feast day: March 2). Ill health resulted in her departure from two religious communities. Founder of the Sisters of the Company of the Cross.

Pauline of the Agonizing Heart of Jesus (born December 16, 1865, in Italy; died July 9, 1942, in Brazil; canonized May 19, 2002; feast day: July 9). As a child, she moved with her family from what is now Italy to Brazil. Brazil's first saint took her removal as superior general with humility and served the poor and her community faithfully in the following thirty-plus years. Cofounder of the Congregation of the Immaculate Conception's Little Sisters.

Rafqa Pietra Choboq Ar-Rayès (born June 29, 1832, in Lebanon; died March 23, 1914, in Lebanon; canonized June 10, 2001; feast day: March 23). She offered up her suffering, including eventual blindness and paralysis. Sister with Lebanon's Maronite Order of the Blessed Virgin Mary.

María Josefa Sancho de Guerra (born September 7, 1842, in Spain; died March 20, 1912, in Spain; canonized October 1, 2000; feast day: March 20). People told her they didn't think she had a vocation as a woman religious. So she established her own community. Founder of the Servants of Jesus of Charity.

1. https://www.irmadulce.org.br/english/religious/
   phrases-and-prayer

2. http://w2.vatican.va/content/john-paul-ii/en/homilies/2000/
   documents/hf_jp-ii_hom_20000409_beatifications.html

3. http://w2.vatican.va/content/john-paul-ii/en/homilies/2000/
   documents/hf_jp-ii_hom_20000409_beatifications.html

4. http://w2.vatican.va/content/john-paul-ii/it/homilies/1994/
   documents/hf_jp-ii_hom_19941016_beatificazione.html

5. http://www.santiebeati.it/dettaglio/90319

6. https://www.papalencyclicals.net/Pius10/p10por.htm

7. *Fatima in Lucia's Own Words.* Father Louis Kondor, SVD,
   editor. July 2007 edition. p. 44. https://web.archive.org/
   web/20160409203714/http://www.pastorinhos.com/_wp/
   wp-content/uploads/MemoriasI_en.pdf

8. *Fatima in Lucia's Own Words.* Father Louis Kondor, SVD,
   editor. July 2007 edition. P. 59. https://web.archive.org/
   web/20160409203714/http://www.pastorinhos.com/_wp/
   wp-content/uploads/MemoriasI_en.pdf

9. Elizabeth of the Trinity, Sister. *The Complete Works, Volume 2:
   Letters from Carmel*, p.351. Translated by Anne Englund Nash.
   ICS Publications: Washington, D.C. 2014.

10. http://w2.vatican.va/content/john-paul-ii/fr/homilies/1984/
    documents/hf_jp-ii_hom_19841125_nuovi-beati.html.

11. Elizabeth of the Trinity, Sister. *The Complete Works, Volume 2:
    Letters from Carmel*, p.332. Translated by Anne Englund Nash.
    ICS Publications: Washington, D.C. 2014.

12. https://www.nobelprize.org/prizes/peace/1979/
    teresa/26200-mother-teresa-acceptance-speech-1979/.
13. https://www.govinfo.gov/content/pkg/CREC-1994-05-02/
    html/CREC-1994-05-02-pt1-PgS16.htm.
14. https://www.govinfo.gov/content/pkg/CREC-1994-05-02/
    html/CREC-1994-05-02-pt1-PgS16.htm.
15. https://www.piercedhearts.org/purity_heart_morality/mother_
    teresa_address_united_nations.htm.
16. https://www.govinfo.gov/content/pkg/CREC-1994-05-02/
    html/CREC-1994-05-02-pt1-PgS16.htm.
17. http://www.vatican.va/news_services/liturgy/saints/
    ns_lit_doc_20000409_beat-Hesselblat_en.html.
18. http://www.sainteuphrasia.com/home/inner/15.
19. http://www.vatican.va/content/francesco/en/homilies/2013/
    documents/papa-francesco_20130512_omelia-canonizzazioni.
    html.
20. https://madrelaura.org/santa-laura-montoya-/127/cod21/
21. Schäffer, Anna. *Thoughts and Memories of My Life of Illness and
    My Longing for the Eternal Homeland.* Edited by Georg Franz
    X. Schwager. Regensburg, Germany: Verlag Schnell & Steiner
    GmbH, 2012, p. 12.
22. Hanley, Sister Mary Laurence, O.S.F., and O.A. Bushnell.
    Pilgrimage and Exile: Mother Marianne of Moloka'i. Honolulu,
    HI: Mutual Publishing, 2009, p. 39.
23. http://www.saintmariannecope.org/quotes_note.html.
24. https://www.sosj.org.au/our-foundress-mary-mackillop/
    marys-story/mary-story-fulfilment/.
25. http://www.vatican.va/content/john-paul-ii/en/homilies/1986/
    documents/hf_jp-ii_hom_19860208_stadio-kattayam.html.

26. http://alphonsa.net/i-am-like-one-lying-transfixed-to-the-cross/.

27. http://www.vatican.va/content/john-paul-ii/en/homilies/2004/documents/hf_jp-ii_hom_20040516_canonizations.html.

28. https://saintgianna.org/marriproposal.htm.

29. https://www.aciprensa.com/noticias/hoy-se-celebra-a-santa-maravillas-de-jesus-de-la-orden-de-las-carmelitas-descalzas-90480.

30. http://www.vatican.va/news_services/liturgy/saints/ns_lit_doc_20030504_torres-morales_en.html.

31. http://w2.vatican.va/content/john-paul-ii/en/homilies/2001/documents/hf_jp-ii_hom_20011125_canonization.html.

32. http://w2.vatican.va/content/john-paul-ii/en/homilies/2001/documents/hf_jp-ii_hom_20011125_canonization.html.

33. https://www.xula.edu/mainabout.

34. https://www.bakhitacharities.org/saint-bakhita-quotes.

35. Ewald, Daniel P., Father. *Saints and Blesseds of the Americas.* 2009. Bloomington, IN: Xlibris Corp. p. 121.

36. *Diary of St. Maria Faustina Kowalska: Divine Mercy in My Soul.* 3rd edition, 2019. Marian Press, Stockbridge, MA. 1107.

Franciscan Media is a nonprofit ministry of the Franciscan Friars of St. John the Baptist Province. Through the publication of spiritual books, *St. Anthony Messenger* magazine, and online media properties such as *Saint of the Day, Minute Meditations,* and *Faith & Family,* Franciscan Media seeks to share God's love in the spirit of St. Francis of Assisi. For more information, to support us, and to purchase our products, visit franciscanmedia.org.

A NONPROFIT MINISTRY OF THE FRANCISCAN FRIARS

ABOUT THE AUTHOR

Melanie Rigney is the author of several books, including *Sisterhood of Saints: Daily Guidance and Inspiration.* She also writes for *Catholic Digest, Living Faith,* CatholicMom.com, Women in the New Evangelization, and other sites and publications. She lives in Arlington, Virginia.